# 123 Creative Marshmallow Recipes

*(123 Creative Marshmallow Recipes - Volume 1)*

Wendy Beran

Copyright: Published in the United States by Wendy Beran/ © WENDY BERAN

Published on December, 07 2020

All rights reserved. No part of this publication may be reproduced, stored in retrieval system, copied in any form or by any means, electronic, mechanical, photocopying, recording or otherwise transmitted without written permission from the publisher. Please do not participate in or encourage piracy of this material in any way. You must not circulate this book in any format. WENDY BERAN does not control or direct users' actions and is not responsible for the information or content shared, harm and/or actions of the book readers.

In accordance with the U.S. Copyright Act of 1976, the scanning, uploading and electronic sharing of any part of this book without the permission of the publisher constitute unlawful piracy and theft of the author's intellectual property. If you would like to use material from the book (other than just simply for reviewing the book), prior permission must be obtained by contacting the author at author@sauterecipes.com

Thank you for your support of the author's rights.

# Content

## 123 AWESOME MARSHMALLOW RECIPES .................................................. 5

1. BROWN BUTTER RICE KRISPIE TREATS .................................................. 5
2. Bacon Berry S'mores Pie .................. 5
3. Banana Hot Chocolate ..................... 6
4. Brown Butter Marshmallow Popcorn ..... 6
5. Brown Butter Rice Krispie Balls W Smoked Almonds & Cap'n Crunch Ganache ..... 6
6. Brown Butter–Bourbon Rice Krispies Treats .................................................. 7
7. Burnt Cinnamon Toast & Chocolate S'more 8
8. Candied Sweet Potatoes With Walnuts, Cranberries, And Marshmallowettes ..... 8
9. Champagne Marshmallow Treats ........ 8
10. Chartreuse Rice Krispies ................... 9
11. Chocolate Chip Biscuit S'mores .......... 9
12. Chocolate Covered Marshmallows ..... 9
13. Chocolate Creamsicle Pie .................. 10
14. Chocolate Rocky Road Ice Cream ..... 11
15. Cinnamon Spice Rice Krispies Treat S'mores ................................................ 11
16. Coconut Crispy Treat ........................ 12
17. Coconut Sweet Potato Casserole ....... 12
18. Coffee Creme De Cacao Dessert ....... 13
19. Coffee Toffee Crispy Treats With Chocolate Chips .................................... 13
20. Cookies And Cream Rice Krispie Squares 14
21. Curried Coconut Cashew Rice Krispies Treats .................................................. 14
22. DARK, CREAMY, RICH, CHOCOLATE FUDGE .................................................. 14
23. Dairy Free Rocky Road Ice Cream ..... 15
24. Double Chocolate Fudge ................... 15
25. Easy Almond Bars ............................. 15
26. Everything Cookie Ice Cream Sandwich .. 16
27. Flourless Salted Hot Chocolate Cookies .. 16
28. Frozen Sun Gold Cherry Tomato Cheesecake ........................................... 17
29. Fruit & Nut Chocolate Fudge ............. 18
30. Fruit And Marshmallow Icebox Tart ... 18
31. Fruit And Nut Cereal Bar ................... 19
32. Golden Oreo Rice Krispies Treats ...... 19
33. Gourmet Rocky Road .......................... 20
34. Grandma Joan's Marshmallow Brownies .. 20
35. Grilled Banana Boats .......................... 21
36. Grilled Banana With Chocolate & Crushed Peanut Brittle ........................................ 21
37. Harvest Squash Surprise ..................... 22
38. Hersey Bar Pie/Tart .............................. 22
39. Homemade Hostess Cupcakes ............ 23
40. Homemade Moon Pies! ....................... 24
41. Honey Marshmallow Crème Swirl Dark Chocolate Chunk Cookies .................... 25
42. Hostess Cupcakes ................................ 26
43. Hot Cocoa Cake With Peppermint Marshmallow Frosting ............................ 27
44. Hot Chocolate Ice Cream With Torched Marshmallows ......................................... 28
45. Iced Oatmeal Pie Bars .......................... 29
46. Inside Out Sweet Potato Casserole ....... 29
47. Kickin' Rocky Road Popcorn ................ 30
48. Lamington A La Fondue ....................... 30
49. Lemon Meringue Pie Ice Cream ........... 31
50. Marshmallow Creamy Yogurt ............... 32
51. Marshmallow Trio (Peppermint, Vanilla Rose, And Chocolate Fudge) ................. 32
52. Marshmallow Bars ................................ 33
53. Matcha Whoopie Pies ........................... 33
54. Mexican Chocolate Cookies With Marshmallow Frostin .............................. 34
55. Meyer Lemon Italian Ice Tiramisu Tart .... 34
56. Mimi's Sweet Potato Casserole ............. 35
57. Mint Chocolate Rice Krispies Treats ...... 35
58. Mississippi Mud Chocolate Cheesecake .... 35
59. Mississippi Mud Chocolate Cheesecake Recipe .................................................... 36
60. Modjeskas ............................................ 37
61. New Zealand Lolly Cake ........................ 37
62. Nutella S'Mores ..................................... 38
63. Passover Rocky Road ............................ 38
64. Peanut Butter Banana S'more Sliders ..... 38
65. Peanut Butter Cheerio Bars With M&M's 39
66. Peanut Butter Clusters ........................... 39
67. Peanut Butter And Jelly Crispy Brown Rice Bars 40
68. Peanut Butter Cereal Treats ................... 40
69. Peppermint Marshmallow Hot Chocolate Cookies .................................................. 40

70. Peppermint Rice Krispies Treats ................ 41
71. Popcorn Toasted Cereal Cake .................... 42
72. Pumpkin Marshmallow Toffee Cookies ... 42
73. Pumpkin Spie Latte Macaron Cookies ...... 43
74. Pumpkin Whoopie Pies With Maple Cream Filling ............................................................... 44
75. Quisp Cereal, Candied Bacon And Marshmallow Cookie ........................................ 45
76. Red Velvet Milkshake ..................................... 45
77. Rice Crispies And Mixed Nut Balls .......... 45
78. Rocky Road ....................................................... 46
79. Rocky Road Potato Chip Bites ................... 46
80. Rocky Road Toffee ......................................... 47
81. Russian Bird`s Milk Cake Ice Cream ......... 47
82. S'Mores Brownie Ice Cream Sandwiches .. 48
83. S'mores Bark .................................................... 49
84. S'mores Brownies ........................................... 49
85. S'mores Cheesecake ....................................... 50
86. S'mores Chocolate Tart ................................. 50
87. S'mores Cookies .............................................. 51
88. S'mores Croissants ......................................... 52
89. S'mores Fridge Cake ...................................... 53
90. S'mores Ice Cream .......................................... 53
91. S'mores Icebox Cake ...................................... 54
92. S'mores Layer Cake ........................................ 54
93. S'mores Pie ....................................................... 55
94. S'mores Pop Tart Slab Pie ............................ 56
95. S'mores Cake ................................................... 58
96. Sally's S'Mores ................................................. 58
97. Salted Toffee & Brown Butter Crispy Treats 59
98. Sheet Pan S'mores .......................................... 60
99. Spooky Halloween Popcorn Balls .............. 60
100. Spumoni Rocky Road .................................. 61
101. Strawberry Cheesecake Rice Krispie Treats 62
102. Strawberry S'mores Sundae ........................ 62
103. Stuffed With Fluff Mars Bar Cupcakes ..... 63
104. Swedish Princess Cake ................................ 64
105. Sweet Cherries & Creme Puffs .................. 65
106. Sweet Potato Sinfulness .............................. 65
107. Sweet Potato Soufflé .................................... 66
108. Sympathy For The Devil's Food Cake ...... 67
109. S'MORES SKILLET ...................................... 68
110. S'Mores Pudding Cake ................................ 68
111. S'more Cookie Cups ..................................... 69
112. S'mores Angel Food Cake ........................... 70

113. S'mores Cookie Dough Bites ...................... 70
114. THE BEST BANANA BUTTERSCOTCH ICE CREAM EVER .................................................. 71
115. The Best Chocolate Brownies From Scratch 72
116. Tropical Ambrosia ......................................... 72
117. Vanilla Marshmallow Creme Brulee .......... 72
118. Vegan Rocky Road Ice Cream ................... 73
119. Vegetable ......................................................... 73
120. Wagon Wheel Slice ....................................... 74
121. Waldorf Salad ................................................ 74
122. White Chocolate Rocky Road .................... 75
123. Fluffer Nutter Brownies .............................. 75

**INDEX** ....................................................... **77**
**CONCLUSION** ........................................... **79**

# 123 Awesome Marshmallow Recipes

***

## 1. BROWN BUTTER RICE KRISPIE TREATS

*Serving: Makes about 20 square-ish treats | Prep: | Cook: | Ready in:*

### Ingredients

- 1/2 cup butter, plus extra for pan
- heaping 1/4 teaspoons sea salt or pink Himalayan salt (be generous)
- 1 10-ounce bag mini marshmallows (6 cups)
- 6 cups Rice Krispies (about 1/2 a 12-ounce box)

### Direction

- Thoroughly butter a baking sheet.
- In a large pot, melt butter over medium to medium-low heat. It will melt, then foam, then turn clear golden and finally start to turn brown and smell nutty. Add sea salt. Stir frequently, scraping up any bits from the bottom as you do. Don't take your eyes off the pot as while you may be impatient for it to start browning, the period between the time the butter begins to take on colour and the point where it burns is often less than a minute.
- As soon as the butter takes on a nutty color, reduce heat to low and stir in the marshmallows. Continue stirring until marshmallows are melted and smooth.
- Remove the pot from the stove and gently fold in the cereal, until combined. Turn the mixture onto the buttered baking sheet and press flat with your hands. As you press the mixture together, create an outside edge with a spatula.
- Let cool, cut into squares and listen up for the "Mmmm-ing".

## 2. Bacon Berry S'mores Pie

*Serving: Serves 6 | Prep: | Cook: | Ready in:*

### Ingredients

- 1 9 inch graham cracker pie crust
- 4 ounces Semi-Sweet Chocolate Chips
- 10 ounces mini marshmallows
- 1/2 cup strawberries
- 1/2 cup blueberries
- 6 slices bacon

### Direction

- Melt the chocolate in a microwave safe bowl 30 seconds at a time, until fully melted.
- Pour melted chocolate into piecrust and spread evenly.
- Put 1/2 of the marshmallows on top of the melted chocolate and put in a 350-degree oven for 5 minutes
- While the pie is in the oven, cook the bacon till crisp. Then crumble.
- Remove pie from the oven and pat softened marshmallows down to form a flat, even surface.
- Slice strawberries and lay over marshmallows.
- Spread blueberries over strawberries.
- Spread crumbled bacon over blueberries
- Top with the remaining marshmallows.
- Return the pie to the oven for 5 minutes, or until top is nicely browned.

## 3. Banana Hot Chocolate

*Serving: Serves 2 | Prep: | Cook: | Ready in:*

### Ingredients

- 2 ripe bananas
- 2 cups vanilla almond milk (unsweetened)
- 1-2 tablespoons unsweetened cocoa powder
- Mini Marshmallows
- Ground Cinnamon

### Direction

- Place bananas and almond milk in a blender and puree until smooth
- Strain banana and milk mixture into a small sauce pot
- Over medium heat, slowly warm up the banana milk mixture until hot, but not boiling
- Add unsweetened cocoa powder and whisk until well combined. For a strong cocoa flavor add 2 tbsp. cocoa powder
- Pour into mugs and top with marshmallows and ground cinnamon

## 4. Brown Butter Marshmallow Popcorn

*Serving: Serves 4-6 | Prep: | Cook: | Ready in:*

### Ingredients

- 1/2 cup unsalted butter
- 1/2 vanilla bean
- 10 ounces mini marshmallows
- 1 teaspoon kosher salt
- 9 cups popped popcorn (unpopped kernels removed)

### Direction

- In a large pot, melt the butter on low heat.
- Split the vanilla bean in half lengthwise, and scrape out the seeds. Add to the melted butter. Continue to cook the butter on low until the milk solids start to brown.
- Remove from heat, add the salt and mini marshmallows and stir to combine. Return the pot to low heat and stir to completely melt the marshmallows.
- Once the marshmallows have completely melted, add the popcorn and stir to combine.
- Line a baking dish with parchment paper and spray with baking spray. Pour the popcorn into the dish and allow to cool.

## 5. Brown Butter Rice Krispie Balls W Smoked Almonds & Cap'n Crunch Ganache

*Serving: Makes about 45 balls | Prep: | Cook: | Ready in:*

### Ingredients

- Brown Butter Rice Krispie Balls w Smoked Almond
- 1 cup Cap'n Crunch Ganache
- 1 cup Cap'n Crunch, very finely chrushed.
- 1 Stick Unsalted Butter
- 1 bag marshmallows (if you are using fancy ones you'll need about 40)
- 1 teaspoon Vanilla paste or Seeds from 1 Vanilla Bean
- 2 teaspoons Smoked Salt
- 5 cups Rice Krispies
- 1 cup Chopped Smoked Almonds
- 4 ounces Melted Super Dark Chocolate
- Cap'n Crunch Cereal Milk Ganache
- 2 cups Cap'n Crunch (reg or peanut butter)
- 3/4 cup Heavy Cream or Light Cream orr 1/2 & 1/2
- 10 ounces Dark Chocolate, chopped
- 1 teaspoon unsalted butter

### Direction

- Brown Butter Rice Krispie Balls w Smoked Almond
- Roll Ganache into @ 45 balls (1 teaspoon-ish each) and roll each one in Cap' Crunch Dust, place on plate/cookie sheet & refrigerate...this will make things so much easier down the line
- Pre-Heat oven to 375Pour rice krispies on to a cookie sheet and toast @ 15 minutes until they are fragrantly toasty, and a few shades darker than they were before
- Place Butter in Saucepan over extremely low heat and melt slowly till it starts to smell nutty and turn brown, depending on your pot this can take anywhere from 15 minutes (calphalon saucepan) to 25 (regular saucepan). Stir, shake pan occasionally. Don't let it burn!
- Remove butter from heat & stir in vanilla.
- Place Marshmallows on a lined cookie sheet and toast in over until they get brown and toasty as well.
- Scrape Marshmallows into to a large Sauce pan over very low heat, add butter/vanilla & salt stir well to combine.
- Add Rice krispies & Almonds Continue stirring until it becomes a large sticky smoky salty mass remove from heat and spread out in cookie sheet or transfer to bowl
- Take about a Tablespoon of Krispie treat roll in to a ball, make and indentation with your thumb and jam the ganache ball in there, close up the ball, using more krispie treat if required....repeat ...a lot
- Drizzle melted balls with melted Dark Chocolate, let cool & enjoy.
- IF you do not feel like making the ganache, Nutella is a fabulous substitute.
- Cap'n Crunch Cereal Milk Ganache.
- You can make this a few days ahead of the Rice Krispie treats and store in fridge.
- Preheat oven to 375, Place cereal on a cookie sheet and toast in oven until fragrant (@ 5-10 minutes).
- Place cereal in a bowl, pour cold cream over and let sit @ 20 -30 minutes.
- Strain cream into sauce pan, mushing all the cereal bits with a ladle to get all the liquid out.
- Heat cream slowly over low until it comes to simmer.
- Pour hot cream over chopped chocolate, stir with rubber spatula until chocolate has melted & cream have combined, stir in butter.
- Pour into shallow dish and cool until malleable.

## 6. Brown Butter–Bourbon Rice Krispies Treats

*Serving: Serves 24 | Prep: 1hours5mins | Cook: 0hours15mins | Ready in:*

### Ingredients

- 2 sticks (1 cup) salted butter, plus more for greasing
- 3 (12-ounce) bags mini marshmallows, divided
- 1/4 cup bourbon
- 1 tablespoon vanilla extract
- 1/4 teaspoon kosher salt
- 10 cups (one 12-ounce box) rice cereal, such as Rice Krispies
- Flaky sea salt, to garnish

### Direction

- Grease a 9x13-inch baking pan with butter. Set aside.
- In a very large pot set over medium-high heat, melt butter, stirring constantly, until the milk solids at the bottom of the pan start to brown and the butter smells nutty and darkens in color. This will take about 5 minutes. Do not walk away or leave unattended.
- As soon as the butter has browned, add two bags of marshmallows, the bourbon, vanilla, and salt. Cook for 5 to 6 minutes, stirring constantly, until the mixture is golden, smells like caramel, and is smooth and glossy.
- Turn off the heat, add the remaining bag of marshmallows, and stir just until melted. Add the rice cereal and quickly stir to coat them

with the marshmallow mixture. (If your pot is not big enough, quickly transfer the mixture into the largest mixing bowl you have.)
- Transfer into the prepared baking pan and gently press into an even layer. If the mixture is too sticky, coat your hands in butter or oil to make it easier to work with. Garnish with flaky salt. Let cool completely and cut into squares.

## 7. Burnt Cinnamon Toast & Chocolate S'more

*Serving: Makes 4 | Prep: | Cook: | Ready in:*

### Ingredients

- 8 slices cinnamon swirl bread
- 4 chocolate marshmallows (store-bought or homemade)
- Dark chocolate
- Flaky sea salt

### Direction

- Turn on the broiler. Lay 8 slices of cinnamon swirl bread on a parchment-lined baking sheet. Broil until more than toasted, even a little black in spots.
- Flip the slices over, put a square of chocolate on 4 of the slices and a marshmallow on the other four, then broil until the chocolate is melt and the marshmallow is toasty (or burnt — whatever you like).
- Sprinkle a flaky salt on the melted chocolate, then top with the marshmallow-toast. Gobble. This s'more can also be made over a fire, of course.

## 8. Candied Sweet Potatoes With Walnuts, Cranberries, And Marshmallowettes

*Serving: Serves 10-12 | Prep: | Cook: | Ready in:*

### Ingredients

- 8 medium sweet potatoes
- 4 tablespoons butter
- 1 cup dark brown sugar
- 3/4 teaspoon salt
- 1/4 teaspoon black pepper
- 1 teaspoon nutmeg
- 1/2 cup white grape juice
- 1/2 cup walnuts
- 1/2 cup whole cranberries
- 1/2 cup mini marshmallows

### Direction

- Preheat oven to 350°F.
- Peel the potatoes and cut them into 2" disks. Place them in a large pot with enough water to cover and cook until boiling; reduce the heat, cover and simmer for about 10 minutes or so, until the potatoes are fork tender. Drain, and place in a large oven-proof casserole dish.
- Melt the butter and brown sugar in a small saucepan, and stir in the salt, pepper, nutmeg, and grape juice. Pour the mixture over the potatoes.
- Arrange a walnut, a cranberry or two, and a marshmallow in and around each potato for decorative effect.
- Bake for 50 – 60 minutes. Remove from oven and serve immediately.

## 9. Champagne Marshmallow Treats

*Serving: Makes 8 to 10 treats | Prep: | Cook: | Ready in:*

### Ingredients

- 6 tablespoons (85 g) unsalted butter
- 1/4 cup (59 ml) dry champagne
- 6 cups (318 g) mini marshmallows
- 1/2 teaspoon vanilla extract
- 1/4 teaspoon kosher salt
- 6 cups (192 g) crisped rice cereal

## Direction

- Line a 9 x 9-inch (23 x 23-cm) baking dish with foil. Spray with non-stick cooking spray and set it aside.
- In a large skillet preheated to medium heat, melt the butter. Add the champagne, stir and let it simmer for about minute. Next, add the marshmallows, vanilla extract and kosher salt. Stir the marshmallows until completely melted, or about 4 minutes.
- Remove the skillet from the heat and add-in the cereal. Stir to combine. Pour the mixture into the prepared baking dish. Press the mixture into the dish and let it cool completely before slicing it and serving!
- Variation: Throw caution to the wind and try these treats with rosé or white wine!

## 10. Chartreuse Rice Krispies

Serving: Makes 1 batch | Prep: | Cook: | Ready in:

## Ingredients

- 2 tablespoons unsalted butter, rom temp.
- 3/4 cup green Chartreuse
- Pinch kosher salt
- 8 ounces marshmallows
- 4 cups rice krispies

## Direction

- Grease a 9 x 5 pan with butter (or line with parchment and grease).
- In a medium saucepan, add the Chartreuse and simmer for about 10 minutes, until it reduces by 75%. Then add the butter and salt and stir until melted.
- Add the marshmallows and stir until melted. Turn off the heat and stir in the cereal until well-mixed. Pour into the prepared pan and cool.

## 11. Chocolate Chip Biscuit S'mores

Serving: Serves 8 | Prep: | Cook: | Ready in:

## Ingredients

- 3 cups Bisquick Mix
- 1 cup Milk
- 1 1/2 Bags of Milk Chocolate Chips
- 8 Large Marshmallows

## Direction

- Heat oven to 450
- Add 3 cups of Bisquick mix into a large bowl
- Pour 1 cup milk over the mix and combine
- Knead 10 times on a floured surface
- Add 1 ½ bags of milk chocolate chips into dough and knead. Pull apart dough into 8 large balls and place onto cookie sheet
- Bake for 7-9 minutes until the biscuits are golden brown. Remove and let cool
- Pull each biscuit apart in the center and place 1 jumbo marshmallow in the middle
- Place back in the oven for about 3 minutes so the marshmallow will become toasted and gooey! Enjoy your Chocolate Chip Biscuit S'mores!!

## 12. Chocolate Covered Marshmallows

Serving: Makes 24-30 | Prep: | Cook: | Ready in:

## Ingredients

- 24 large marshmallows
- 8 ounces white chocolate, chopped
- Chocolate sprinkles

### Direction

- Place chopped chocolate in a microwave-safe bowl. Microwave on high in 20 second intervals until chocolate is melted. Stir in the oil until well combined.
- Drop marshmallows, one at a time, into the melted chocolate, using a spoon or a fork to be sure marshmallow are completely covered on all sides. Lift the chocolate covered marshmallows one at a time with a fork and place on waxed paper or parchment paper. Sprinkle with chocolate sprinkles while chocolate is still soft.
- Allow chocolate to harden, at least 2-3 hours. To speed up process, place in the fridge to harden. Store in the fridge until ready to eat.

## 13. Chocolate Creamsicle Pie

*Serving: Serves 8 - 10 | Prep: | Cook: | Ready in:*

### Ingredients

- For the crust:
- 30 Oreo cookies
- 4 tablespoons butter, softened to room temperature
- 2 tablespoons butter, melted
- For the filling:
- 3-1/2 ounces mini marshmallows (approx. 3 cups)
- 1/3 cup whole milk
- 3 tablespoons orange marmalade
- 1-1/2 teaspoons finely grated orange zest (about 1 large orange)
- 2 teaspoons vanilla extract
- 5 bunches Cointreau
- 1 tablespoon orange juice, freshly squeezed
- 1-1/2 cups heavy cream
- Gel food coloring - red (1-2 drops) & yellow (3-4 drops) (optional)
- orange zest, for garnish (optional)

### Direction

- Start the crust by pulverizing the Oreos in a food processor until they're a fine rubble. Drop in the soft butter and continue to blitz. While the blade is running pour in the melted butter and continue to process until it's all well incorporated.
- Tumble this mixture out into a fluted tart pan with a removable bottom and press it evenly across the bottom and up the sides. Place in the fridge while you start the filling.
- Mix the marshmallows and milk in a medium saucepan and place over low heat. Stir regularly until it all melts together—about 5 - 7 minutes.
- Once melted, pour the liquidated marshmallow into a heatproof dish.
- Beat in the marmalade, orange zest and juice, Cointreau and vanilla extract and set aside until it is completely cooled.
- Once the marshmallow mix is completely cooled whip the cream in a standup mixer with the whisk attachment on medium speed until medium-stiff peaks form—about 4 - 5 minutes.
- Turn the mixer down to low and pour in the cooled marshmallow mix and beat just until combined.
- Scrape down the bottom and sides with a rubber spatula to make sure it's all evenly incorporated.
- If you're using the food coloring add this in now and whisk just until combined.
- Pour the filling into the crust and cover lightly with foil, as not to mar the top, and refrigerate for at least 8 hours, but preferably overnight.
- Decorate the top with extra orange zest, fine or in long strips, just before serving if you want—either way, this is delicious!
- -You can make this up to two days in advance and just keep it in the fridge.-You can also make it ahead and freeze it; lay the pie in the

freezer, flat and unwrapped, until it's frozen solid. Then wrap in two layers of plastic wrap and freeze for up to 2 months. To defrost, unwrap it and cover it lightly with foil and place in the fridge for 8 hours.

## 14. Chocolate Rocky Road Ice Cream

*Serving: Serves 4 | Prep: | Cook: | Ready in:*

## Ingredients

- 200 milliliters whole milk
- 380 milliliters heavy cream
- 215 grams sugar
- 1 pinch salt
- 3 teaspoons cornstarch
- 50 grams cream cheese
- 20 grams cocoa powder
- 25 grams vanilla marshmallows
- 30 grams dark chocolate
- 45 grams roasted smoked almonds

## Direction

- For the caramel ripple sprinkle 100gr sugar evenly over the bottom of a heavy-duty 4-quart saucepan, set it over low heat and cook barely stirring only when the inner layer of sugar starts to melt, mix the liquefied sugar with the crystallized sugar on top of it very gently. Don't over stir. When all of the sugar is liquefied, continue cooking on low stirring until the caramel is penny-bronze in color. Take off heat, slowly add 180ml heavy cream a little at a time, stirring constantly until fully incorporated. If there are any lumps of hardened caramel left, return to low heat and stir until completely melted. Take off heat, add a pinch of salt, cool to room temperature and store in a sealed jug until ready to use.
- For the chocolate sauce in a small saucepan combine 80ml water, 45gr sugar and sifted unsweetened cocoa powder, cook on medium 2-3min until smooth. Take off heat, add the chopped dark chocolate, leave to fully dissolve, then return to medium heat, stir until smooth and take off heat.
- Dissolve the cornstarch in 50ml whole milk, leave to rest.
- For the ice cream base in another saucepan combine the leftover milk, 200ml heavy cream, 70gr sugar and a pinch of salt, stir, place on medium heat, bring to an almost boil, add the cornstarch milk and cook constantly stirring until thickened. Take off heat, add the cream cheese and the chocolate sauce, mix until glossy and smooth. Cool to room temperature, then transfer into the fridge overnight.
- Freeze in your ice cream maker according to the manufacturer's instructions, adding mini marshmallows and chopped almonds at the last couple of minutes of churning. Transfer into an airtight container, swirling in pockets of the caramel sauce (use half the amount that you prepared) and store in the freezer for at least 4 hours until firm enough to scoop.

## 15. Cinnamon Spice Rice Krispies Treat S'mores

*Serving: Makes 10 s'mores | Prep: 0hours0mins | Cook: 0hours0mins | Ready in:*

## Ingredients

- 4 tablespoons butter (half a stick)
- 4 cups mini marshmallows, almost one full 10-ounce bag (snack on the rest, resistance is futile)
- 1 teaspoon cinnamon
- 1/2 teaspoon nutmeg
- 6 cups puffed rice cereal (do your thang if you wanna use that expen$ive bougie brown rice stuff, I judge you not)
- 10 regular-sized marshmallows
- 2 cups semi-sweet chocolate chips

## Direction

- Melt butter in a pot over medium heat, and then add mini marshmallows, cinnamon, and nutmeg, stirring with a heat-proof spatula until the entire mixture is melted.
- Remove pot from heat and add cereal, folding in until the whole mess is coated and gooey and sticky.
- Dump contents of pot into a rimmed baking sheet coated with cooking spray. Mine is 15 x 10 inches, and I used a baking sheet rather than a dish because I wanted thinner krispies treats on either side of my s'more so it was still possible to fit the whole thing vertically in my mouth. I have priorities. Flatten into one layer with your spatula, and then stick the dish into the freezer for at least 15 minutes.
- Remove baking sheet from freezer and cut into 20 rectangles. Return to freezer for 5 minutes.
- Using a skewer or similarly longish utensil, roast the big marshmallows over your stove burner, or a campfire, or a candle, or whatever you have nearest that is engulfed in flames. Smash roasted mallow between two krispies treats, pressing together to form a sandwich. Repeat with remaining mallows and treats.
- Heat chocolate in the microwave, stopping to stir every 15 seconds, until melt and smooth. Dip krispies sandwiches halfway into the chocolate, and then place onto a sheet of wax paper. Stick sandwiches into the fridge to speed along the hardening process. Try to save one for your boyfriend but just in case maybe don't tell him you made them so after you've eaten them all, he is none the wiser.

## 16. Coconut Crispy Treat

*Serving: Serves 12 | Prep: | Cook: | Ready in:*

### Ingredients

- Coconut butter
- 4 cups shredded coconut (unsweetened)
- Coconut Rice Crispies
- 4 cups brown rice crispies
- 10 ounces marshmallows
- 1 tablespoon unsalted butter
- 2 tablespoons coconut butter
- 3/4 cup toasted coconut

### Direction

- Coconut butter
- Using a large nonstick pot, over medium-high heat, toast all four cups of the shredded coconut. While toasting, make sure to stir frequently so coconut doesn't burn. The coconut is done when it changes to golden brown and smells fragrant.
- Set coconut aside to cool.
- Once coconut has cooled, reserve 3/4 of a cup for the treats. Place the remainder in the bowl of a food processor. Process until smooth. It should take about 5-8 minutes of solid processing to develop a silky consistency. Set coconut butter aside.
- Coconut Rice Crispies
- Grease a 13 by 9 pan. Set aside.
- In a large pot, over medium-high heat, melt butter. Then add marshmallows. When marshmallows are just about melted, stir in the 2 TBSP of coconut butter. Remove from heat.
- To marshmallow mixture, add rice crispies and toasted coconut. Mix until coated.
- Spread mixture into greased pan. Let cool. Cut and enjoy.

## 17. Coconut Sweet Potato Casserole

*Serving: Serves 4 to 6 | Prep: | Cook: | Ready in:*

### Ingredients

- 3 pounds sweet potatoes (about 3 large), peeled and cut into 1-inch chunks
- Kosher salt
- 1/2 cup unsweetened coconut cream
- 3 tablespoons unsalted butter
- 1 tablespoon peeled, finely grated ginger root

- A pinch or two of freshly grated nutmeg
- Freshly ground black pepper
- 2 cups mini or regular marshmallows
- 2 tablespoons unsweetened, shredded coconut

## Direction

- Preheat oven to 375° F.
- Place sweet potatoes in a pot and cover with water by 1-inch, salt water generously. Bring to a boil, then reduce to a simmer and cook until tender, about 15-20 minutes. Drain and return potatoes to the pot. Add the coconut cream, butter, ginger, and nutmeg. Mash until smooth, and season generously with salt and pepper. Transfer to a 2-quart baking dish. Top with marshmallows and coconut. Bake until the marshmallows and coconut are lightly browned, about 15 to 20 minutes. Serve immediately.

## 18. Coffee Creme De Cacao Dessert

*Serving: Serves 8-10 | Prep: | Cook: | Ready in:*

### Ingredients

- 1 cup chopped walnuts
- 1 cup Milk
- 8 ounces marshmallows
- 2 cups whipping cream
- 1/2 cup Creme De Caco
- 1 tablespoon Instant Coffee
- Walnut halves for garnish

### Direction

- Butter a 9-inch square pan and sprinkle with chopped walnuts.
- Melt the marshmallows in milk over hot water; remove from heat to cool.
- Whip cream and fold into marshmallow mixture.
- Fold in Crème DeCacao and instant Coffee.
- Pour into pan and decorate with walnut halves.
- Chill overnight.
- Cut into squares to serve.
- Refrigerate leftovers.

## 19. Coffee Toffee Crispy Treats With Chocolate Chips

*Serving: Serves 4 | Prep: | Cook: | Ready in:*

### Ingredients

- 8 cups crispy rice cereal
- 1 1/2 cups toffee bits
- 1 cup mini chocolate chips
- 4 tablespoons butter
- 3 tablespoons finely ground instant coffee or espresso powder
- 1 packet 16 oz. mini marshmallows

### Direction

- Grease a 9x12 pan, or use parchment paper sprayed with non-stick cooking spray. The parchment paper will lift out of the pan.
- In a large bowl, mix rice cereal with toffee chips and chocolate chips. Mix until chips are distributed evenly throughout.
- In a medium pan on medium low heat, melt the butter and add the coffee. Stir until coffee is dissolved. Add the marshmallows and stir until melted...don't let them burn!
- Fold the butter, coffee and marshmallow mixture into the rice cereal mixture. Stir until completed combined.
- Transfer mixture into the prepared pan. Pat down the top until even.
- Let cool and cut into squares. Some of the chips will melt and some will stay intact. They taste great, especially with a cup of coffee.

## 20. Cookies And Cream Rice Krispie Squares

*Serving: Makes 24 squares | Prep: | Cook: | Ready in:*

### Ingredients

- 1/2 cup butter
- 1 10 oz) package regular marshmallows
- 2 cups mini marshmallows
- 7 cups Rice Krispie Cereal
- 2 1/2 cups coarsely chopped Oreo Cookies
- 3 (1.55 oz) Hershey's Cookies 'n' Cream Candy Bars, chopped
- 1/2 cup chopped Oreo Cookies, for topping

### Direction

- 1) Melt butter in large saucepan over low heat. Add regular marshmallows and stir until melted and well-blended. Cook 2 minutes longer, stirring constantly. Remove from heat.
- 2) Add Rice Krispies. Stir until well coated. Fold in the mini marshmallows, chopped Oreos and chopped Cookies 'n' Cream Candy Bars.

## 21. Curried Coconut Cashew Rice Krispies Treats

*Serving: Makes 9-10 dozen | Prep: | Cook: | Ready in:*

### Ingredients

- 3 tablespoons coconut oil
- 2 tablespoons Madras curry powder (yellow curry)
- 1/2 teaspoon salt
- 1 10-ounce bag marshmallows
- 1/2 teaspoon vanilla extract
- 3/4 cup unsweetened coconut flakes, lightly toasted
- 1/2 cup cashews, toasted and coarsely chopped
- 5 cups Rice Krispies Cereal

### Direction

- Lightly grease a 9×13-inch pan with coconut oil.
- In a large saucepan melt 3 tablespoons of coconut oil over low heat. Add curry, salt, and marshmallows and stir until the marshmallows are completely melted. Remove from heat.
- Add vanilla, coconut, cashews, and rice cereal. Stir until well coated.
- Using lightly oiled hands or waxed paper evenly press the mixture into the prepared pan. Let cool at room temperature.
- Cut into 1-inch squares and serve.

## 22. DARK, CREAMY, RICH, CHOCOLATE FUDGE

*Serving: Serves 2 1/2 pounds | Prep: | Cook: | Ready in:*

### Ingredients

- 2 1/2 cups white sugar
- 1/2 cup sweetened condensed milk
- 1/2 cup water
- 1/2 cup butter
- 12 oz bittersweet chocolate pieces or chips (I used Guittard)
- 6 ounces mini marshmallows
- 1 tsp vanilla extract
- 1 1/2 cups roughly chopped walnuts

### Direction

- In a large pot add the sugar, sweetened condensed milk, water and butter. Stir until the mixture boils and makes a soft ball when dropped in a glass of water. (This happens rather quickly!)
- Remove from the heat and add the vanilla.
- Quickly beat the chocolate and the marshmallows into the mixture until they have dissolved completely. Then add the walnuts and mix thoroughly.

- Spread the mixture on a slab of marble or a baking sheet and let it cool.
- After the fudge is completely cooled, cut it into whatever size pieces that you want.

## 23. Dairy Free Rocky Road Ice Cream

*Serving: Serves 4-6 | Prep: | Cook: | Ready in:*

### Ingredients

- 2 cups coconut milk
- 1 cup almond milk
- 3/4 cup coconut sugar or honey
- 1/3 cup cocoa powder
- 1 teaspoon sea salt
- 1/2 cup marshmallows, chopped
- 1/2 cup walnuts, chopped

### Direction

- In a mixing bowl, combine milks, sugar, cocoa and salt. Blend until sugar has dissolved.
- Pour into an ice cream machine and churn according to directions.
- Once ice cream has finished churning, pour into a large bowl and stir in marshmallow pieces and walnuts.
- Scoop into bowls or cones and serve.

## 24. Double Chocolate Fudge

*Serving: Makes 5 pounds | Prep: 0hours0mins | Cook: 0hours0mins | Ready in:*

### Ingredients

- 4 cups granulated sugar
- 12 ounces can evaporated milk
- 8 ounces semi-sweet chocolate
- 8 ounces unsweetened chocolate
- 7 ounces marshmallow creme
- 3/4 cup butter @ room temperature
- 2 teaspoons vanilla extract
- 2 cups nuts (optional)

### Direction

- In a heavy saucepan over medium heat, combine sugar and milk. Bring to a boil for 6 minutes, stirring occasionally.
- Remove from heat and add chocolates, marshmallow cream, butter, vanilla and nuts.
- Stir until all ingredients are well mixed.
- Pour into a greased 9 x 13 inch pan and refrigerate until firm. Cut into squares.
- Yields 5 pounds of fudge.

## 25. Easy Almond Bars

*Serving: Makes 24 bars | Prep: | Cook: | Ready in:*

### Ingredients

- 1/4 cup unsalted butter
- 2-3 dashes salt
- 10 ounces marshmallows
- 2 teaspoons almond extract
- 8 cups corn flakes cereal
- 1/2 cup sliced almonds

### Direction

- Line a 9 x 13 inch pan with foil or parchment, and oil or butter the lining. Spray or butter a large, heat-resistant spoon or spatula.
- Melt butter in a large pot over medium heat until it barely becomes brown; quickly turn heat to low. Move the pot to coat its inner walls with the butter.
- Add marshmallows and let them melt, stirring occasionally. Just when marshmallows are smooth, turn off heat; stir in extract and salt.
- Add cornflakes alternately with almonds; mix until all are coated, then quickly pour into prepared pan.

- Press down with buttered spoon or hands to make even. Cool and slice.

## 26. Everything Cookie Ice Cream Sandwich

*Serving: Makes 6 giant sandwiches | Prep: | Cook: | Ready in:*

### Ingredients

- 1 cup  all-purpose flour
- 2 teaspoons  baking soda
- 1/2 teaspoon  salt
- 2 teaspoons  finely ground coffee
- 1/3 cup  crushed original hickory sticks
- 1 cup  crushed corn flakes
- 1/3 cup  crushed pretzels
- 1/4 cup  crushed pecans
- 1/3 cup  rolled or instant oats
- 1 cup  mini marshmallows
- 2 tablespoons  sesame seeds
- 2/3 cup  dark chocolate chips
- 1/2 cup  butter
- 2 tablespoons  duck fat (or more butter)
- 1/2 cup  dark brown sugar
- 1/2 cup  granulated sugar
- 2 teaspoons  vanilla extract
- 1  large egg
- 6 cups  of your favorite ice cream

### Direction

- In a bowl, whisk together the flour, baking soda, salt and ground coffee.
- To crush the hickory sticks, corn flakes, pretzels and pecans, I placed them in the bowl of a food processor and pulsed a few times. If you don't have a food processor you can also place the ingredients in a ziplock bag wrapped in a towel and crush them with a rolling pin. Transfer to a separate bowl and add oats, marshmallows, sesame seeds and chocolate chips. Toss to mix.
- If your butter is still cold, cut it in cubes of 1-2 cm and heat it in the microwave 10 seconds at a time until softened but not melted. Place the butter, duck fat and both types of sugar in the bowl of a stand mixer or in a big bowl with a hand mixer. Beat on medium-high speed for 3 minutes or until light and fluffy. Add the vanilla extract and the egg and mix for 30 seconds or until the mixture is smooth and uniform.
- Add the flour mixture to the bowl and beat on low speed until there is no more dry ingredients. Top with the rest of the ingredients (hickory sticks, corn flakes, pretzels, pecans, oats, marshmallows, sesame seeds, chocolate chips) and continue mixing, still on low speed, to blend them in evenly.
- Cover the bowl with plastic wrap and place the dough in the fridge for an hour, so that it can firm up and will be easier to roll into cookies.
- 15 minutes before you take the dough out, heat the oven to 350°F. Cover two baking sheets with a Silpat or parchment paper. Place 2 tbsp. of dough per cookie in your hands and roll them into a ball. Place a maximum of 6 cookies per sheet. They will spread quite a lot.
- Bake for 12-15 minutes, until the edges are golden brown and the middle is set. Let them completely cool.
- Scoop 1 cup of ice cream on a cookie and top with a second one, now enjoy!

## 27. Flourless Salted Hot Chocolate Cookies

*Serving: Makes 6-8 cookies | Prep: | Cook: | Ready in:*

### Ingredients

- 2 1/2 cups  confectioner's sugar
- 1/2 cup  dutch pressed unsweetened cocoa powder
- 1 teaspoon  cinnamon

- 1/2 teaspoon cardamom
- 1 teaspoon espresso powder
- 1/4 teaspoon sea salt (for batter)
- 3 large egg whites, room temperature
- 1 teaspoon pure vanilla extract
- 4 ounces semi-sweet chocolate
- 4 ounces bittersweet chocolate
- 1/2 cup mini marshmallows
- 1 teaspoon sea salt (for topping)

## Direction

- Preheat oven to 350 degrees F. Grease a parchment-lined baking sheet. In a medium bowl, sift together confectioner's sugar, cocoa powder, cinnamon, cardamom, 1/4 tsp sea salt, and espresso powder. Combine thoroughly with spoon.
- Add egg whites and vanilla and stir until dough forms. Add semi-sweet and bittersweet chocolate, cut into thick chunks, and the marshmallows.
- Using an ice cream scoop, form 6-8 mounds on your baking sheet. Don't press down – the mounds will spread out into cookie form in the oven. Bake for 15 minutes, until the tops crackle. Let cool at least 10 minutes before serving.
- Enjoy; I know you will. These are ideal with a glass of ice cold milk, or vanilla bean or coffee gelato.

## 28. Frozen Sun Gold Cherry Tomato Cheesecake

*Serving: Serves 12 | Prep: | Cook: | Ready in:*

## Ingredients

- 1 3/4 cups cake flour
- 1/4 teaspoon salt
- 1 teaspoon baking powder
- 1/2 cup plain yogurt
- 1 stick unsalted butter
- 1 cup plus 2/3 cup plus 2 tablespoons granulated sugar
- 1 teaspoon vanilla extract
- 2 large eggs, separated
- 1/2 cup plus 2 tablespoons cocoa powder
- 2/3 cup boiling water
- 2/3 cup bittersweet chocolate, chopped
- 2 1/2 cups halved Sun Gold cherry tomatoes plus more for garnish
- 1 tablespoon fresh lemon juice
- 12 oz cream cheese
- 1 3/4 cups marshmallow fluff
- 3/4 cup plus 1 1/2 cups heavy cream

## Direction

- Heat oven to 350 degrees F. Grease 9-inch spring form pan.
- In a bowl, sift together flour, salt and baking powder. Add yogurt; mix until well combined.
- In a separate bowl, using an electric mixer, beat butter, 1 cup sugar and vanilla until light and fluffy. Add egg yolks, one at a time, beating well after each addition. Beat in flour mixture a little at a time; beat until well combined.
- In a separate bowl, using an electric mixer, beat egg whites until stiff peaks form. Gently fold egg whites into batter.
- Place 1/2 cup cocoa in a separate bowl. Pour boiling water over cocoa and whisk until all lumps are dissolved. Add bittersweet chocolate to cocoa and stir until melted. Gently fold chocolate mixture into batter.
- Pour cake batter into pan. Batter should be about 1 inch high. Bake 25 minutes or until a toothpick inserted comes out clean. Remove and cool completely on wire rack.
- Clean pan and return cooled cake to pan top side down. Line the inside edges of pan with a long strip of parchment paper that extends 2 inches above rim. Make sure parchment sleeve is tight against cake edge so cheesecake filling doesn't run down side. Tape parchment to secure. Transfer pan to freezer while preparing filling.

- Puree cherry tomatoes, 2/3 cup sugar and lemon juice in food processor until smooth; set aside. In a bowl, beat cream cheese until smooth. Mix in marshmallow fluff. In separate bowl, whip ¾ cup heavy cream until stiff peaks form; stir into cream cheese mixture. Gently fold in cherry tomato puree.
- Remove cake from freezer and pour filling over top. Return to freezer for overnight (or at least 8 hours).
- Several hours before serving, whip 1 ½ cups heavy cream, 2 tablespoons cocoa powder and 2 tablespoons sugar to soften peaks. Dollop on top of cake. Freeze again. Allow cake to sit at room temperature for 15 minutes before using a hot knife to slice and serve. Garnish top with halved cherry tomatoes dusted in sugar.

## 29. Fruit & Nut Chocolate Fudge

*Serving: Makes 20 squares | Prep: 0hours0mins | Cook: 0hours0mins | Ready in:*

### Ingredients

- 200 milliliters evaporated milk
- 100 milliliters full cream milk
- 1 cup light brown sugar
- 1/2 cup mini marshmallows
- 150 grams dark chocolate, chopped
- 50 grams butter
- 1/2 teaspoon vanilla extract
- 50 grams macadamia nuts, roughly chopped
- 50 grams almonds, roughly chopped
- 100 grams dried cranberries

### Direction

- Grease a 20cm square cake tin and line the base with baking paper.
- Put the evaporated milk, full cream milk, sugar and marshmallows in a deep saucepan over a low heat. Stir continuously until the sugar has dissolved and the marshmallows have melted.
- Bring the mixture to the boil. Allow to boil for 12 minutes, stirring continuously until the mixture has reached soft ball stage. To test this, simply drop a small amount of syrup into a bowl of ice water. If you are able to roll the syrup into a soft ball then you are good to go!
- Take the pot off the heat. Add the dark chocolate, butter and vanilla extract and mix well until the butter and chocolate have melted. Mix in the chopped macadamias, almonds and cranberries.
- Working quickly, tip the mixture into the prepared tin. Use a spatula to gently flatten the top, (it does not have to be completely smooth).
- Pop the tin into the fridge for 3-4 hours until firm. Cut the fudge into blocks and store in an airtight container in the fridge. The fudge will firm up even further overnight.

## 30. Fruit And Marshmallow Icebox Tart

*Serving: Serves 16 | Prep: | Cook: | Ready in:*

### Ingredients

- Graham Cracker Crust
- 1 3/4 cups graham cracker crumbs (about 1 sleeve)
- 1 1/2 sticks unsalted butter, melted
- Marshmallow-Cream Cheese Filling & Glaze
- 4 cups cream cheese, room temperature
- 4 cups marshmallow cream, natural, homemade or vegan preferred
- zest and juice of 2 limes
- 2 cups hulled strawberries, cut into ⅛- to ¼-inch slices
- 2 cups blackberries
- 1/2 cup lime marmalade
- 2 teaspoons water

### Direction

- Make the crust: Place the graham cracker crumbs into the bowl of a food processor, add the butter, and process for about 10 seconds, until smooth, but not paste. This can also be done easily by hand.
- Press the graham cracker mixture in the bottoms and up the sides of 8 (4-inch) mini-tart pans. Refrigerate while you make the filling.
- Make the filling: Spray a mixing bowl with nonstick vegetable oil spray, combine the marshmallow, cream cheese, lime juice, and zest. Blend with a wooden spoon until thoroughly incorporated. Transfer the filling into the chilled graham cracker crusts.
- Arrange the strawberries and blackberries in a decorative pattern on top of the filling.
- Melt the lime marmalade and water in the microwave (for about 10 seconds) or in a small saucepan set over medium heat, and pour through a fine-mesh sieve into a heatproof measuring cup with a spout. Gently pour the glaze over the fruit on the tart and let stand until set. The tarts can be refrigerated and served chilled or at room temperature and is best served the day it is made. The sooner, the better.

## 31. Fruit And Nut Cereal Bar

*Serving: Makes 20 bars | Prep: | Cook: |Ready in:*

### Ingredients

- 5 tablespoons tablespoons unsalted butter
- 7 cups Mini Marshmallows
- 1/2 teaspoon Salt
- 1 teaspoon Vanilla
- 6 cups Fruit-o-Shaped cereal
- 1/2 cup Sliced Almonds
- 1/2 cup Dried Cherries
- 1 cup Greek Yogurt Chips

### Direction

- Line a 9x9 pan with parchment and coat with nonstick spray. Set aside.
- In a large sauce pan, melt the butter over low heat. Add the marshmallows and stir continuously until they are melted. Remove from the heat and stir in the salt and vanilla.
- Pour the cereal into the melted marshmallow and stir to coat.
- Add in dried cherries and almonds and stir to combine.
- Press the mixture into the prepared pan.
- Place the pan in the refrigerator to allow the white chocolate to set, about 20 minutes.
- Cut into bars and dip the bottom of each bar into the Greek yogurt chips. Sit on parchment paper to set up. Once all of the bars are dipped, drizzle more of the Greek yogurt on top, if desired.
- Store in an airtight container at room temp for up to 5 days.

## 32. Golden Oreo Rice Krispies Treats

*Serving: Serves 9 very generously | Prep: | Cook: |Ready in:*

### Ingredients

- Crust
- 25 Golden Oreos, finely crushed
- 4 tablespoons unsalted butter, melted
- Cereal Treats
- 10 Golden Oreos, coarsely chopped
- 1 10 ounce bag mini marshmallows
- 4 tablespoons unsalted butter, cubed
- 3 1/2 cups Rice Krispies

### Direction

- Line an 8 inch square pan with parchment. Make the crust. Place the Oreos in the bowl of a food processor and process until ground into crumbs. Pour into a bowl and stir together with butter until fully coated. Pour into the

prepared pan and press down firmly to form a crust in the bottom of the pan. Refrigerate at least 30 minutes, until firm.
- After the crust has chilled, make the treats. In a large microwave safe bowl, place marshmallows and butter. Microwave on high in 30 second increments, stirring in between to promote melting and prevent burning, until fully melted. Add Oreos and Rice Krispies and stir until fully incorporated. Pour the treat mixture on top of the crust. Spread into an even layer and press down firmly with hands. Refrigerate at least 30 more minutes to set before cutting into bars and serving. Treats may be stored in an airtight container in the refrigerator for up to 5 days, or frozen, wrapped in parchment and foil and placed in a zipper bag for up to 3 months. Thaw at room temperature for about an hour.

## 33. Gourmet Rocky Road

*Serving: Makes approx. 20 | Prep: | Cook: | Ready in:*

### Ingredients

- 40g   whole almonds
- 75g   shelled pistachios
- 250g   rosewater Turkish delight, coarsely chopped
- 200g   marshmallows
- 40g   dried cherries
- 450g   dark chocolate, melted**

### Direction

- Preheat oven to 200C. Toast almonds/pistachios on foil-lined tray in oven 5-8 mins, or until brown. Remove/cool.
- Lightly grease two bar cake tins (8cm x 26cm) and line base and sides with baking paper.
- Combine nuts, Turkish delight, marshmallows and cherries in bowl. Stir well and spoon into prepared tins.

- Pour warm chocolate over marshmallow mixture, tapping tins gently to remove air bubbles.**Note: To melt - break chocolate into small pieces and put into glass bowl over pot of simmering water, without base of bowl touching water. Remove when smooth and glossy.
- Refrigerate until set then cut into 3-4cm pieces. Store in airtight container in the fridge.
- Enjoy!!

## 34. Grandma Joan's Marshmallow Brownies

*Serving: Makes 5 dozen tiny pieces | Prep: | Cook: | Ready in:*

### Ingredients

- For the brownies:
- 4   squares (4 ounces) unsweetened baking chocolate
- 2   sticks salted butter
- 4   eggs
- 2 cups   sugar
- 1 teaspoon   vanilla extract
- 1 cup   sifted flour
- 1 cup   chopped walnuts or pecans (optional)
- Marshmallows (enough to cover the pan)
- For the frosting:
- 2   squares (2 ounces) unsweetened baking chocolate
- 1   stick salted butter
- 3 cups   confectioners' sugar
- 1/4 cup   milk
- 12   marshmallows

### Direction

- Grease a 9- by 13-inch baking pan and heat the oven to 350° F.
- In the top of a double boiler, melt the chocolate and the butter together. Let cool.
- Beat the eggs and the sugar well, then beat in the chocolate mixture and the vanilla extract.

- Add the sifted flour and nuts, if using, and stir until just combined. Pour into prepared pan and bake for 25 to 30 minutes (grandma says, "or more").
- Meanwhile, quarter enough marshmallows to cover the top of the pan.
- When the brownies are almost finished, make the frosting: Melt chocolate, marshmallows, and butter in the top of a double boiler. Add sugar and milk and beat until smooth (grandma says, "Beat until ready").
- Remove baked brownies from the oven and immediately cover with the quartered marshmallows—no need to be dainty. Pour frosting over top and smooth with a nonstick spatula. Allow to cool completely before slicing into small pieces (I like to stick them in the freezer for an hour or so, and I then store them there, in a plastic container, too.)

## 35. Grilled Banana Boats

*Serving: Serves 8 | Prep: 0hours10mins | Cook: 0hours10mins | Ready in:*

### Ingredients

- 8 barely ripe bananas [see note below]
- 1 pound fresh cherries, pitted and halved [may use frozen but thaw to room temperature]
- 8 tablespoons rum [ADULTS ONLY, choose your favorite silver, spiced or aged rum]
- 1 cup chocolate chips
- 2 cups mini marshmallows
- vanilla ice cream [optional garnish]
- whipped cream [garnish]
- chocolate sauce [garnish]
- caramel sauce [garnish]
- chopped nuts [garnish]

### Direction

- Have at the ready 8 pieces of aluminum foil topped with 8 pieces of parchment paper, just large enough to seal over bananas and stuffing.
- Use a small sharp paring knife to almost cut through banana in peel lengthwise starting from stem end to bottom end. Slightly pull peel back to expose banana flesh. Place bananas on top of parchment paper/foil.
- Place two tablespoons each of cherries, chocolate chips and marshmallows inside each slit banana. If making adult version, add 1 tablespoon of rum to each banana.
- Seal parchment/foil over bananas and stuffing, but not too tightly; need to allow for heat expansion. Place foil packets on grill over dying embers or after gas./electricity has been shut off. This can be done after grilling dinner. Leave banana boats on grill for approximately 10 to 20 minutes (or through the end of dinner) to warm through, but turn 2-4 times to allow for even warming and melting of chocolate and marshmallows.
- Remove foil packets from grill and place on paper plates, then use a small sharp paring knife to cut open foil/parchment paper. Garnish to taste with any leftover halved cherries, vanilla ice cream, whipped cream, chocolate sauce, caramel sauce and/or chopped nuts. Serve immediately!
- NOTE #1: It is not recommended to use really ripe bananas as they will fall apart to easily. Barely ripe bananas will hold their shape and integrity better for this recipe.
- NOTE #2: This recipe can be made during cold weather months using your oven. Preheat oven to 425 degrees F and then turn it off. Place foil packets on a baking sheet and place in oven for 10-20 minutes, turning 2-4 times.

## 36. Grilled Banana With Chocolate & Crushed Peanut Brittle

*Serving: Makes 1 grilled banana | Prep: 0hours5mins | Cook: 0hours5mins | Ready in:*

### Ingredients

- 1 tablespoon butter, softened
- 2 tablespoons crushed or chopped peanut brittle
- 2 tablespoons chopped dark chocolate
- 1 ripe banana (you want a yellow or darker banana)
- Ice cream of your choice (optional)

### Direction

- If using a gas grill, heat it for medium direct cooking. If using a charcoal grill, after taking dinner off, add more coals if necessary and close the lid until you're ready to cook. In either case, clean the grates.
- Put the butter, peanut brittle, and chocolate in a small bowl and mash together. Slit the banana from top to bottom along one side, through the top peel but not the bottom peel. Pull the banana open enough so you can push the filling into the slit.
- Put the banana on the grill directly over the fire, slit side up. Close the lid and cook until the peel turns black, about 5 minutes. Transfer to a plate.
- To serve, eat right from the peel or spoon over ice cream, angel food cake, or vanilla pudding.

## 37. Harvest Squash Surprise

*Serving: Serves 6 | Prep: | Cook: |Ready in:*

### Ingredients

- 1 butternut squash peeled, seeded and cubed
- 1 cup cream cheese, dill flavour
- 1/4 cup butter
- 1 lg. egg
- 3 tablespoons finely chopped flat leaf parsley
- 2 cups miniature marshmallows
- 2 teaspoons cinnamon
- salt & pepper to taste

### Direction

- In a pot simmer the squash until fork tender, drain.
- Puree or mash with a fork. Stir in butter, cream cheese, parsley, egg, season to taste with salt & pepper. Spoon into 6 ungreased ramekins. Top with marshmallows. Lightly sprinkle with cinnamon.
- Bake in a preheated 375F oven for 15min. Broil 2-4 min to color marshmallow.
- Watch carefully!

## 38. Hersey Bar Pie/Tart

*Serving: Serves 8-10 | Prep: | Cook: |Ready in:*

### Ingredients

- 1 packet Graham Crackers
- 1/4 cup Clarified Butter- melted
- 8 Hersey Bars - 6 oz size
- 3/4 Bag Large Marshmallows
- 1/4 cup Milk
- 1 1/2 cups Whipped Cream

### Direction

- Place Graham crackers in a small plastic bag seal and crush with a rolling pin until medium fine. Place in a small bowl and add melted butter and mix until well blended. Spread on the bottom and sides of a tart or pie pan but do not press down firmly leave loose.
- In a double boiler place the Milk, Hersey Bars and Marshmallows. Cook until all the ingredients are melted, set aside to cool. Place a paper towel over the pan to help avoid a skin on the mixture.
- Whip the cream. Fold the cream into the cooled chocolate mixture, do not over mix but make sure all is blended well and that there are no large lumps of whipping cream.
- Spoon the chocolate mixture on to the prepared graham crackers and smooth the top.

I spoon a little more of the mixture toward the center to give it a little height in the center of the pie. Cover with plastic wrap and freeze until ready to serve. Remove from freezer about 10 minutes before serving.

## 39. Homemade Hostess Cupcakes

*Serving: Makes 18-20 cupcakes | Prep: | Cook: | Ready in:*

### Ingredients

- The Cupcakes
- 1 1/4 cups unbleached, all purpose flour
- 2 teaspoons baking soda
- 2 teaspoons baking powder
- 1/4 teaspoon salt
- 1 1/4 cups granulated sugar
- 1 cup water
- 4 ounces unsweetened chocolate, chopped
- 4 ounces unsalted butter, room temperature
- 2 teaspoons vanilla extract
- 2 large eggs, lightly beaten
- The Filling, Ganache & Icing Ingredients
- 4 tablespoons unsalted butter, softened
- 1 cup powdered sugar
- 1 teaspoon vanilla extract
- 3 tablespoons heavy cream
- 1 cup marshmallow cream
- 6 ounces bittersweet chocolate, chopped
- 1/2 cup heavy cream
- 1 tablespoon unsalted butter, softened
- 1 teaspoon vanilla extract
- 4 tablespoons unsalted butter, softened
- 1 tablespoon milk
- 1 cup powdered sugar
- 1/4 teaspoon pure vanilla extract

### Direction

- Place oven rack in the center of the oven and preheat oven to 350 degrees.
- Spray muffin tins (18-20 tins) with nonstick bakers spray (or line with paper liners.
- Make the cupcakes. Place the sugar and 1 cup of water in a saucepan. Bring to a boil, stirring until the sugar dissolves, about 3 minutes.
- Pour the sugar into the bowl of an electric mixer and add the chocolate and butter. Let the mixture sit, stirring occasionally, until the chocolate is melted and the mixture has cooled slightly. Stir in the vanilla.
- Sift together the flour, baking soda, baking powder and salt. Set aside.
- Add the eggs, one at a time, to the chocolate mixture, blending on medium speed until well combined.
- Gradually add the flour mixture to the chocolate mixture, on low speed, until the batter is smooth.
- Divide the batter evenly between the prepared muffin tins. Fill each muffin about 1/2 way up (about 1/4 cup batter per cupcake). Bake until a toothpick inserted in the center comes out clean, about 18 to 20 minutes. The cupcakes will sink in the middle slightly. That is okay.
- Cool cupcakes in the pans for 25 minutes, then transfer to a rack to cool completely.
- Make the filling. While the cupcakes are cooling, use an electric mixer to cream 4 Tbsp. of butter until it is light and fluffy. Beat in 1/2 cup confectioners' sugar, then add 1 tsp. of vanilla and 1 Tbsp. of heavy cream. Beat until smooth. Slowly add the remaining 1/2 cup confectioner's sugar and the 2 Tbsp. of heaving cream, alternating between the two ingredients. Beat in the marshmallow cream. Scrape the filling into a small bowl, cover with plastic, and refrigerate until ready to use.
- Make the Ganache. Place the 6 ounces of bittersweet chocolate in a stainless steel bowl. Heat the heavy cream and 1 Tbsp. butter in a sauce pan just until boiling. Pour over the chocolate. Let stand for 5 minutes. Whisk until smooth. Add the 2 tsp. vanilla. Let stand until cool, but still glossy and liquid.
- Fill the cupcakes. Put the cream filling into a pastry bag fitted with a medium star tip. Insert the tip into the center of each cupcake top. Fill until the cupcake feels "heavier" but don't

overfill. It is okay if some of the filling peaks out the top - it will be covered by the ganache.
- Frost the cupcakes. When the ganache has cooled enough to work with, spoon 1 tbsp. onto each cupcake and spread lightly with an offset spatula or knife. Chill for at least 15 minutes.
- Prepare the curly-q icing. Using a mixer, beat the remaining 4 Tbsp. butter with 1/4 tsp. vanilla, 1 Tbsp. milk and 1 cup of confectioner's sugar until smooth. Add more milk if needed. Spoon the icing into a pastry bag fitted with a small tip and pipe on the trademark curly-q. Store cupcakes in the refrigerator.

## 40. Homemade Moon Pies!

*Serving: Makes 16 moon pies | Prep: | Cook: | Ready in:*

### Ingredients

- For the graham cracker cookies and the marshmallow crème:
- FOR THE COOKIES:
- 1 cup brown rice flour
- 1 cup oat flour
- 1 cup almond flour
- 1/4 cup arrowroot powder
- 1/4 cup light brown sugar
- 1/2 teaspoon baking powder
- 1/4 teaspoon salt
- 3/4 teaspoon ground cinnamon
- 3 tablespoons coconut oil, solid
- 1/4 cup almond milk
- 1/4 cup maple syrup
- FOR THE MARSHMALLOW CREME:
- 2 egg whites, room temperature
- 1/4 teaspoon cream of tartar
- 1/2 cup natural cane sugar
- 1/4 cup maple syrup
- 3 tablespoons water
- 1 pinch salt
- 1 teaspoon pure vanilla extract
- To make the chocolate shell and assemble the cookies:
- 6 ounces 60 to 70% bittersweet chocolate
- 1 tablespoon coconut oil

### Direction

- For the graham cracker cookies and the marshmallow crème:
- Start by making the cookies: To a food processor, add the flours, arrowroot, sugar, baking powder, salt, and cinnamon; pulse to mix. Add the solid coconut oil and pulse until mixture is crumbly. Whisk the syrup and almond milk together; with the motor running, pour through the spout of the food processor to distribute evenly. Once the dough has come together to form a ball, gather it and knead it until smooth. Evenly halve dough, flatten into a disk, and wrap each piece in plastic wrap; let the dough chill in the fridge for 30 minutes.
- Preheat oven to 350° F and line two baking sheets with parchment paper. Remove the dough from refrigerator; let it rest for 5 minutes. On a floured surface, roll dough out to a 1/4-inch thickness. Stamp out cookies with a 2 1/2- to 3-inch round cookie cutter and place on prepared baking sheet. Re-roll dough until it has all been used. (If you want, use a fork to make decorative indentations). Bake in the center of your oven for 10 to 12 minutes, rotating halfway through, until the edges are lightly browned. Remove the cookies from oven and let cool completely. (If making ahead, the finished cookies can be stored in a lidded container in the refrigerator for up to 2 days.)
- Make the marshmallow crème: In a large mixing bowl, beat the egg whites and cream of tartar on medium with a hand mixer until soft peaks form, about 1 minute. (If you own a stand mixer, use it here; it makes it all a lot easier later on when you drizzle in the sugary syrup.) Set aside.
- In a medium saucepan, over medium heat, combine the sugar, maple syrup, water, and

pinch of salt; whisk until the sugar and salt have dissolved, then cook the syrup on medium-high heat until your candy thermometer reaches 240° F. (Each time I make this, my thermometer plateaus around the 200° mark, no need to worry if this happens to you -- it'll reach 240° eventually, just be patient.)

- Remove the sugar syrup from heat. With your mixer on medium, slowly drizzle the syrup down the side of your mixing bowl so that you're beating the egg whites and sugar syrup together. When all the syrup has been mixed in, increase the speed of your mixer to high (medium, if you're using a stand mixer) and beat for 5 to 7 minutes, until the crème is stiff and glossy. Transfer it to a container with a fitted lid and let it rest in the refrigerator until cool. (This step can also be done ahead of time if need be.)
- To make the chocolate shell and assemble the cookies:
- Assemble the moon pies. Arrange half the cookies face-down on a large tray. Then spoon marshmallow crème into a pastry bag (or a large plastic bag with the corner snipped) and distribute an even layer of crème on each one. Gently place another cookie on top of the crème, and allow the sandwiches to rest in the fridge while you prepare the chocolate shell.
- Place the chocolate in a medium heat-proof bowl over simmering water. Allow the chocolate to melt, stirring every so often with a rubber spatula until it's completely melted. Add the coconut oil and mix until combined. Set aside for a few moments to allow the chocolate to cool a bit.
- Prepare a work surface with parchment paper and remove the sandwiches from refrigerator. Using a large spoon, drop one half of the sandwich into the chocolate, turn it over so it's completely coated, and place it on the prepared parchment. Repeat with remaining sandwiches. Allow chocolate to harden.
- To store, line a lidded container with parchment paper and layer paper between each layer of cookies. Store Moon Pies in the refrigerator for up to 4 days.

## 41. Honey Marshmallow Crème Swirl Dark Chocolate Chunk Cookies

*Serving: Makes 24-27 cookies | Prep: | Cook: |Ready in:*

### Ingredients

- honey marshmallow crème
- 2 egg whites, room temp.
- 1/2 cup honey
- 1/4 cup water
- 3/4 cup granulated sugar
- 1/4 teaspoon salt
- 1/2 teaspoon almond extract
- cookies
- 1 1/2 cups all-purpose flour
- 1 teaspoon baking powder
- 1/4 teaspoon baking soda
- 1 teaspoon ground cinnamon
- 1/4 teaspoon salt
- 1/2 cup unsalted butter, softened to room temp.
- 1 cup dark brown sugar, tighly packed
- 2 egg yolks
- 1 egg
- 1/2 teaspoon almond extract
- 12 ounces dark chocolate, chopped
- 1/2 batch honey marshmallow crème (recipe above)
- 1/2 tablespoon sea salt, for sprinkling

### Direction

- Prepare honey marshmallow crème; place egg whites in bowl of a stand mixer. Using the whisk attachment, beat on med-high speed until soft peaks form; set aside. (Leave everything attached, you will be using the mixer again.)

- In a medium-size heavy-bottom saucepan, combine honey, water, sugar, and salt. Bring to a boil, stirring just till sugar has dissolved. Cook till mixture reaches 240 F. on a candy thermometer.
- Set stand mixer on low speed. Slowly drizzle about 2-3 Tablespoons of the cooked sugar mixture into egg whites. Continue slowly streaming in hot sugar mixture (don't add too much at once or the egg whites will scramble). When all the sugar has been added, increase mixer to med-high speed and whip until marshmallow fluff is stiff + glossy (about 5-8 minutes). Add almond extract and beat to combine.
- Cover bowl tightly or place in airtight container, refrigerate until ready to use. {Note; well covered, the marshmallow fluff can be stored about five days in fridge.}
- Prepare cookie dough; in a medium-size bowl, whisk together the flour, baking powder, baking soda, cinnamon and salt; set aside.
- In the bowl of a stand mixer, fitted with paddle attachment, beat together the butter and sugar until creamy + smooth (about 5 minutes on medium speed). Add egg yolks and egg, one at a time, beating for about one minute after each addition - scrape down sides of the bowl as needed. Add almond extract and beat till combined. On low speed, beat in the flour mixture until just blended (try not to overmix). Remove paddle attachment and use a large rubber spatula or wooded spoon to stir in chopped chocolate.
- Remove marshmallow fluff from fridge and add about half to the cookie dough. Gently fold fluff into the dough but do not overmix, you want to see the fluff peeking through the dough. Cover bowl and refrigerate overnight, or for at least 8 hours. Cover remaining marshmallow fluff for later use.
- Preheat oven to 375 F. Line baking sheets with parchment paper.
- For each cookie measure out a rounded Tablespoonful of dough. Arrange cookies on prepared sheet, allowing for about 1 1/2-inches of spreading room. Use the bottom of a measuring teaspoon to make a small indentation in each cookie (don't go all the way through to the bottom). Dollop a small amount of reserved marshmallow fluff into each indentation. {Note; at this point you can either leave the clump of fluff atop cookies, or use a small offset spatula to gently swirl it through the dough.} Sprinkle cookies with a little bit of sea salt.
- Bake 10-12 minutes or until edges are just beginning to turn golden brown. Do Not Overbake. Even though they appeared slightly under baked at first, my cookies were perfect after 10 minutes.
- Remove sheet from oven and allow cookies to rest for about 8-10 minutes or until firm enough to transfer to cooling rack. {{Note; use remaining marshmallow fluff to make sandwich cookies, or combine with peanut butter to create fluffernutters!!}}

## 42. Hostess Cupcakes

*Serving: Makes 18 cupcakes | Prep: | Cook: | Ready in:*

### Ingredients

- For the Cupcakes and Filling
- 2 sticks   salted butter, softened
- 2 cups   granulated sugar
- 2   large eggs
- 1 cup   natural cocoa powder, such as Hershey's Baking Cocoa
- 2 1/2 cups   all-purpose flour
- 1 teaspoon   baking soda
- 1/4 teaspoon   salt
- 1/2 cup   whole milk
- 1 cup   marshmallow fluff
- 1/3 cup   salted butter, softened
- 1/2 cup   powdered sugar
- For the Frosting and Decoration
- 1/3 cup   heavy cream
- 1 cup   bittersweet chocolate morsels
- 1 1/2 tablespoons   salted butter, softened

- 1/2 stick  unsalted butter, softened
- 1/2 cup  powdered sugar

## Direction

- Preheat the oven to 350°F. Line a 6- and 12-muffin tin with paper liners.
- Make the cupcake batter: In the bowl of a heavy-duty stand mixer, cream the 2 sticks of butter and the granulated sugar together at medium speed just until light and fluffy, about 1 minute. Add the eggs, one at a time, and mix just until combined. In a measuring cup, stir 1/2 the cup of hot water and the cocoa together until smooth. Add the cocoa mixture to the butter mixture and mix on low speed for an additional 10 seconds.
- In a medium bowl, whisk together the flour, baking soda, and salt. With the mixer on low speed, gradually add the flour mixture to the butter mixture in batches alternating with the milk, beginning and ending with the flour and beating after each addition until the ingredients are just blended.
- Fill each prepared muffin cup half full with chocolate batter. Bake for 22 to 25 minutes, or until a toothpick inserted in the middle comes out clean. Let cool completely on a wire rack.
- Make the filling: Using a clean bowl and a stand mixer or an electric hand mixer, beat the marshmallow fluff, the 1/3 cup butter, and the 1/3 cup of powdered sugar together until combined and fluffy, about 1 minute. Using the handle of a small fork or spoon, make a hole in the top center of each cake. Gently rotate the utensil in each hole to create a small cavity at each opening. Transfer the filling to a piping bag and pipe in just enough marshmallow mixture to fill each hole. As with the Twinkie, you want a firm grasp on your cupcake as you infuse it with the filling, so as not to allow it to explode; once you feel it growing in size, stop infusing. Use a wet fingertip or the back of a spoon to tamp down any marshmallow peaks, ensuring that the filling is even with the top of the cupcake.
- Make the frosting: In a small saucepan, heat the cream over medium heat until bubbles form at the edges. Add the chocolate morsels and remove the pan from the heat, stirring until the chocolate melts. Add the 1 1/2 tablespoons of butter and continue to stir until smooth. Let cool for three minutes. Transfer the chocolate to a large deep glass bowl. Dip the top of each cupcake into the chocolate to coat, letting the excess chocolate drip back into the bowl. Let the cupcakes rest on a wire rack set over newspapers until the chocolate is set, about 30 minutes.
- Make the frosting decoration: In a small bowl, beat the 1/4 cup butter and the 1/2 cup of powdered sugar together until smooth, about two minutes. Transfer the frosting to a piping bag and decorate the top of each cupcake with a curlicue pattern. Serve immediately. Store in an airtight container for up to 2 days.

## 43. Hot Cocoa Cake With Peppermint Marshmallow Frosting

*Serving: Serves 8-10 | Prep: 0hours30mins | Cook: 1hours0mins | Ready in:*

## Ingredients

- For the cake
- 1 1/4 cups  flour
- 1/2 cup  cocoa powder
- 1/2 teaspoon  baking powder
- 1/2 teaspoon  baking soda
- 1/2 teaspoon  salt
- 1 cup  sugar
- 3/4 cup  milk
- 1  egg
- 1/4 cup  canola oil
- For the peppermint-marshmallow topping & chocolate ganache
- 3  egg whites
- 3/4 cup  sugar

- 1/2 teaspoon salt
- 1/2 teaspoon cream of tartar
- 1 drop peppermint extract
- 1/4 cup heavy cream
- 1/2 cup milk chocolate chips

## Direction

- For the cake
- Preheat oven to 350°F. Grease one 9-inch round cake pan with butter and dust with flour, shaking out any excess. Place a round of parchment in the bottom of the cake pan. Set aside.
- In a large mixing bowl, sift together flour, cocoa powder, baking powder, baking soda, and salt. Add in the sugar and whisk the ingredients together. Make a well in the center of the dry ingredients and add the milk, egg, and oil. Using an electric hand mixer, mix the batter together on a low speed until well combined. Pour the batter into the prepared cake pan and place into the oven. Bake for 30 minutes or until a toothpick comes out clean when inserted into the center of the cake. Remove to a cooling rack.
- Once cool, remove the cake from the cake pan. Peel the parchment paper off the bottom of the cake and put onto a serving plate.
- For the peppermint-marshmallow topping & chocolate ganache
- For the Peppermint-Marshmallow: In a medium glass bowl whisk together egg whites, sugar, salt and cream of tartar. Place the bowl over a pot of simmering water and let the mixture cook, whisking occasionally, for 10 minutes or until the sugar dissolves and the mixture becomes fairly warm. Pour the warm mixture into the bowl of a stand mixer fitted with a whisk attachment and whip on high for 10 minutes or until fluffy and has the consistency of marshmallow fluff. Add a drop of peppermint extract and mix until just combined. Taste and add more extract, if needed.
- When you're ready to serve, dollop the marshmallow over top of the cake and spread with an offset spatula, leaving a 1/2-inch border around of the cake. Alternatively, you can put the marshmallow into a piping bag fitted with a star tip to make a festive design.
- For the Ganache: Heat the heavy cream in a small saucepan over medium heat. Once the cream is warm, remove the pan from the heat and stir in the chocolate chips mix until smooth.
- To serve, pour the warm ganache over top of the cake. Serve immediately. The marshmallow and chocolate will melt together a bit. It's messy, but fun! For a less messy (but equally fun) serving option, slice the cake, plate individually and then drizzle some ganache over top of the slice.

## 44. Hot Chocolate Ice Cream With Torched Marshmallows

*Serving: Serves 4 | Prep: | Cook: | Ready in:*

## Ingredients

- 200 milliliters whole milk
- 200 milliliters heavy cream
- 115 grams sugar
- 1 pinch salt
- 3 teaspoons cornstarch
- 50 grams cream cheese
- 20 grams cocoa powder
- 30 grams dark chocolate
- 45 grams vanilla marshmallows

## Direction

- Using a culinary torch toast mini vanilla marshmallows. Alternatively use a gas hob or a candle. Either way be careful not to burn yourself.
- For the chocolate sauce in a small saucepan combine 80ml water, the unsweetened cocoa powder and 45gr sugar, cook on medium 2-3min until smooth. Take off heat, add the dark chocolate, leave to fully dissolve, then return

- to medium heat, stir until smooth and take off heat.
- Dissolve the cornstarch in 50ml whole milk, leave to rest.
- For the ice cream base in another small saucepan combine the heavy cream, the leftover milk, 70gr sugar, pinch salt, stir, place on medium heat, bring to an almost boil, add the cornstarch milk and cook stirring constantly until thickened. Take off heat, add the cream cheese and the chocolate sauce, mix until smooth and combined. Cool to room temperature, then transfer to the fridge overnight.
- Freeze in your ice cream maker according to the manufacturer's instructions adding the torched marshmallows at the last couple of minutes of churning. Store in an airtight container or spoon right away.

## 45. Iced Oatmeal Pie Bars

*Serving: Makes 9 medium bars | Prep: | Cook: | Ready in:*

## Ingredients

- For the bars
- 1/2 cup (4 ounces) butter
- 1 teaspoon cinnamon
- 1/2 teaspoon nutmeg
- 1/4 teaspoon ginger
- 1/4 teaspoon cloves
- 1 egg
- 1 cup (7 1/2 ounces) brown sugar, lightly packed
- 2 tablespoons molasses
- 2 teaspoons vanilla extract
- 1/2 teaspoon salt
- 1 cup (3 1/8 ounces) quick-cooking oats
- 3/4 cup (3 1/8 ounces) all-purpose flour
- For the frosting
- 1/2 cup (4 ounces) butter, softened
- 1 1/4 cups (5 ounces) confectioners' sugar
- 7 ounces marshmallow cream (fluff)
- 1 teaspoon vanilla extract
- 1/2 teaspoon salt

## Direction

- In a large skillet or saucepan, melt the butter over medium heat. Swirl it constantly until the butter begins to brown and dark solids appear--it will start to quickly smell nutty. Remove it from the heat and whisk in all the spices, then set aside to let cool to room temperature.
- Preheat the oven to 350 degrees F. Butter an 8" x 8" baking pan (I like to line it with parchment for good measure).
- Add the egg, brown sugar, molasses, vanilla, and salt to the cooled butter and beat until light in color and well-mixed.
- Fold in the oats and the flour. Pour the batter into your prepared pan and bake for 25 minutes. Remove from the oven and let cool while you prepare your frosting.
- Beat the softened butter until fluffy, then add the confectioners' sugar and keep beating until pale in color.
- Add the marshmallow cream, vanilla, and salt and beat until light and fluffy.
- Spread over the bars, cut into squares, and serve!

## 46. Inside Out Sweet Potato Casserole

*Serving: Serves 12 | Prep: 0hours0mins | Cook: 0hours0mins | Ready in:*

## Ingredients

- 12 Large Round Sweet Potatoes
- 1 teaspoon Good Olive Oil
- 3/4 cup Unsalted, Room Temperature Butter
- 3/4 cup Light Brown Sugar
- 3/4 cup All-Purpose Flour
- 1/4 teaspoon Ground Cinnamon
- 1/8 teaspoon Ground Nutmeg

- 1/4 teaspoon Real Vanilla Extract
- 1 cup Toasted Pecan Pieces
- 1 cup Small Marshmallows
- Salt and Pepper to Taste

### Direction

- Preheat to 400 degrees.
- Wash the sweet potatoes and scrub well. Place the sweet potatoes on a baking sheet lined with parchment paper and cook for 45 minutes.
- In a large bowl mix together the brown sugar, butter, and flour until crumbly. Add the cinnamon, nutmeg, vanilla extract, pecan pieces. Fold together to combine.
- Remove sweet potatoes from the oven and let rest for 15 minutes until cool enough to work with. Reduce oven to 250 degrees.
- Slice the top and bottom of the sweet potatoes so they can sit up on their own. Scoop out the meat out of the sweet potatoes and place in a reserve bowl.
- Add olive oil, salt and pepper to sweet potato mixture in the reserve bowl.
- Place a few marshmallows in the bottom of the sweet potato shells. Place sweet potato mixture in a pastry bag and squeeze evenly into the sweet potato shells.
- Once filled, press your thumb into the center of each sweet potato and fill the hole with the brown sugar streusel topping you mixed together earlier. Top the streusel with a few marshmallows.
- Place completed stuffed sweet potatoes back in the oven for 10 - 15 minutes, until marshmallows are browned on the top. Remove and serve immediately.

## 47. Kickin' Rocky Road Popcorn

*Serving: Makes 10-12 cups | Prep: | Cook: |Ready in:*

### Ingredients

- 8 cups freshly popped popcorn; no salt (I popped 1/3 cup of kernals)
- 1 1/2 cups unsalted almonds; chopped
- 3/4 cup sugar
- 1/4 cup light corn syrup
- 1/4 cup cocoa powder
- 1 tablespoon instant espresso powder
- 1 teaspoon cinnamon
- 1/4 teaspoon salt
- 1/8-1/4 teaspoons cayenne pepper
- 1/2 cup butter
- 1 teaspoon vanilla extract
- 2 cups mini marshmallows

### Direction

- Preheat the oven to 250 degrees. Oil two 10x14 baking dishes.
- Place popcorn and chopped almonds into a large bowl and set them aside. In a medium saucepan combine the sugar, corn syrup, cocoa powder, instant espresso powder, cinnamon, salt, cayenne pepper, and butter. Bring the mixture to a boil over medium-high heat. Boil for two minutes, until the sugar is melted. Stir in the vanilla, then pour the mixture over the popcorn and almonds. Mix it up until everything is evenly coated. Spread the popcorn into the prepared pans.
- Bake in the oven for 30 minutes, stirring every 10 minutes.
- Remove from the oven and mix in the mini marshmallows. Allow to come to room temperature. Break it into small clumps, and store in an airtight container.

## 48. Lamington A La Fondue

*Serving: Makes enough to go around | Prep: | Cook: |Ready in:*

### Ingredients

- Lamington a la Fondue

- Sponge cake, about an inch+ in height, crusts shaved off and cut into 1X1 inch squares
- 1 - 2 portions of chocolate sauce in a fondue pan
- 1 - 2 ripe bananas, peeled and cut into rings
- 1 - 2 cups of fresh pineapple chunks
- Marshmallows
- Other pieces of fruit, your preference
- 1 - 2 cups of dessicated coconut
- 1 cup of crushed nuts - pistachios, hazelnuts etc
- Optional - liquid food colouring
- Chocolate fondue
- 150g mascarpone cheese
- 3 tablespoons icing sugar, or adjust to taste
- 200g milk/plain/mixed chocolate chips
- 1 - 2 teaspoons vanilla extract
- 1 tablespoon of salted butter
- Enough milk to thin mixture
- Optional: 1 - 2 teaspoons of microplaned orange zest
- Optional: pinch of cinnamon/cardamom powder, to taste

## Direction

- Lamington a la Fondue
- If you want to create some fun, add a couple of drops of food colouring to some of the desiccated coconut to colour it and mix with your hands. Leave it out overnight on a flat plate to 'dry' - you can put it in the oven (not turned on)
- To serve the fondue, put the sponge cake pieces in a bowl, and the other fruit in separate bowls. Set the coconut in bowls as well and then put the warm chocolate into top half of the fondue and light a candle/or turn on the heat source to keep the fondue warm
- Dip a piece of cake or fruit or marshmallow into the chocolate and then into the coconut or nuts, then into your mouth....to eat
- Chocolate fondue
- In a pan, warm the mascarpone cheese on low - medium heat, whisking to loosen. Add the icing sugar and the chocolate chips and whisk till melted and the colour transforms from matte to gloss.
- Once melted, add the vanilla extract and butter then start adding the milk, whisking till you get a slightly thickened pouring consistency. Add the cinnamon/cardamom powder if you like. Keep warm in the fondue pot

## 49. Lemon Meringue Pie Ice Cream

*Serving: Serves 4 | Prep: | Cook: |Ready in:*

### Ingredients

- 200 milliliters whole milk
- 200 milliliters heavy cream
- 165 grams sugar
- 1 pinch salt
- 4 teaspoons cornstarch
- 100 grams vanilla marshmallows
- 45 grams shortbread cookie crumbs
- 125 milliliters fresh lemon juice
- 2 large eggs
- 2 large egg yolks
- 85 grams unsalted butter

### Direction

- For the lemon curd ripple in a small saucepan whisk together the freshly squeezed lemon juice, 80gr sugar, pinch salt, eggs, egg yolks and the unsalted butter, set the pan over low heat whisking constantly until the butter is melted. Cook until thickened, strain through a sieve, cool to room temperature and keep in the fridge until ready to use.
- Dissolve the cornstarch in 50ml whole milk, leave to rest.
- In a small saucepan over medium heat combine the heavy cream, the leftover milk, 75gr sugar, pinch salt, bring to an almost boil, add 100gr either Marshmallow Fluff or plain marshmallows big or small, take the saucepan off the heat and leave until the marshmallows

are completely melted. Then return the saucepan to the medium high, bring to an almost boil once again, add the cornstarch milk and cook constantly stirring until thickened. Take off heat, cool to room temperature, then transfer into the fridge overnight.

- Freeze in your ice cream maker according to the manufacturer's instructions adding the shortbread crumbs at the last couple of minutes of churning. Keep in the freezer until set.

## 50. Marshmallow Creamy Yogurt

*Serving: Serves 2 | Prep: | Cook: | Ready in:*

### Ingredients

- 1 ounce vanilla-flavoured small marshmallows
- 7 raspberry or strawberry yogurt
- 6-8 pieces strawberries or berries of your choice

### Direction

- Place Marshmallows and half of the yogurt in a plastic container and mix well until the yogurt coats the marshmallows. Refrigerate the mixture overnight.
- Take the container out of the fridge. Add the remaining yogurt and halved strawberries, and beat the mixture lightly. Spoon the mixture into each cereal bowl or glass and top it off with strawberries and mint (if you have any).

## 51. Marshmallow Trio (Peppermint, Vanilla Rose, And Chocolate Fudge)

*Serving: Makes about 4-5 dozen 1-inch cubes | Prep: | Cook: | Ready in:*

### Ingredients

- 2 cups sugar
- 2 tablespoons corn syrup
- 1 cup water, divided
- 4 envelopes unflavored gelatin
- 2 egg whites
- 1 pinch salt
- 1 tablespoon vanilla extract (clear imitation for really snow-white marshmallows)
- Confectioner's sugar

### Direction

- Lightly grease an 8x8 square pan, then coat with confectioner's sugar. Set aside.
- Combine sugar, corn syrup, and 1/2 cup water in a large saucepan. Stir over high heat until sugar is dissolved; allow to cook to 250-255 degrees without stirring.
- Meanwhile, combine the gelatin and 1/2 cup water in a small saucepan; allow to sit for 10 minutes, then melt gelatin over low heat until liquefied. Keep in a warm place until ready to use.
- Using a stand mixer, beat egg whites and salt until they're firm but creamy.
- When sugar mixture has reached 250-255 degrees, remove from heat. Promptly stir in gelatin mixture, stirring briskly (gelatin will bubble up - be sure to use a large saucepan!).
- With stand mixer on high speed, stream gelatin mixture slowly into egg whites. Whip on high speed until mixture starts to pull away from sides of the bowl, about 5-8 minutes. Beat in vanilla, then spread quickly in prepared pan and allow to stand for at least 1 hour. Cut into desired shapes and roll in confectioner's sugar.
- FOR PEPPERMINT MARSHMALLOWS: Decrease vanilla to 1/2 tablespoon, and add

- 1/4 tsp. peppermint extract and a dab of green gel color, if desired.
- FOR ROSE MARSHMALLOWS: When adding vanilla, add a scant 1/4 tsp. rose water and a dab of pink gel color, if desired.
- FOR CHOCOLATE FUDGE MARSHMALLOWS: Bring 4 tbsp. water to a boil, then stir in 4 tbsp. unsweetened cocoa. After whipping vanilla into marshmallows, fold cocoa mixture loosely into marshmallows without fully combining. Spread in prepared pan (fudge marshmallows may take a bit longer to set). Roll fudge marshmallows in confectioner's sugar with a bit of cocoa powder added, if desired.

## 52. Marshmallow Bars

*Serving: Serves 3 | Prep: | Cook: | Ready in:*

### Ingredients

- 60 grms   marshmallow
- 20 grms   unsalted butter
- 45 grms   cereal
- 40 grms   almonds

### Direction

- Roast almonds until they are lightly browned. Melt butter in a microwave-safe container (40sec on 500W). Add marshmallow and heat on 500 W for 1 min. Mix well and add cereals and almonds.
- Press mixture into pan.
- I use a glass pie plate for everything and usually double the recipe

## 53. Matcha Whoopie Pies

*Serving: Makes 40 pieces | Prep: | Cook: | Ready in:*

### Ingredients

- Cakes
- 2 cups  all-purpose flour
- 1/2 cup  dutch-process cocoa
- 1 1/4 teaspoons  baking soda
- 1 teaspoon  salt
- 1 cup  buttermilk, well-shaken
- 1 teaspoon  vanilla
- 1/2 cup  unsalted butter, softened
- 1 cup  light brown sugar
- 1  large egg
- Matcha Filling
- 1/2 cup  unsalted butter, softened
- 1 1/4 cups  confectionerary sugar
- 2 cups  Marshmallow Fluff
- 1 teaspoon  vanilla
- 1 tablespoon  ground Matcha powder

### Direction

- Preheat oven to 350°F.
- Whisk together flour, cocoa, baking soda, and salt in a bowl until combined.
- Stir together buttermilk and vanilla in a small bowl.
- Beat together butter and brown sugar in a large bowl with an electric mixer at medium-high speed until pale and fluffy, about 3 minutes in a standing mixer, or 5 minutes with a handheld, then add the egg, beating until combined well.
- Reduce speed to low and alternately mix in flour mixture and buttermilk in batches, beginning and ending with flour, scraping down side of bowl occasionally, and mixing until smooth.
- Spoon or pipe mounds of batter about 2 inches apart on baking sheets. (I used silpats for these, you can butter the baking sheets or use parchment). Bake in upper and lower thirds of oven, switching position of sheets halfway through baking, until the tops are puffed and the cakes spring back when touched, 11 to 13 minutes if you make them large, 8-10 minutes if smaller. Transfer with a metal spatula to a rack to cool completely.
- Make filling: Beat together butter, confectioners' sugar, marshmallow, Matcha

powder, and vanilla in a bowl with electric mixer at medium speed until smooth, about 3-5 minutes.
- Assemble pie: Spread or pipe filling on flat sides of half of the cakes, and top with remaining cakes. For a large pie, use up to a tablespoon of filling, for the mini pies, use a teaspoonful.

## 54. Mexican Chocolate Cookies With Marshmallow Frostin

*Serving: Makes 15 cookie sandwiches | Prep: | Cook: | Ready in:*

### Ingredients

- Chocolate Cookies
- 16 ounces semi sweet chocolate, chopped
- 1/4 cup butter
- 1 1/3 cups sugar
- 4 eggs
- 1 teaspoon vanilla extract
- 3/4 cup flour
- 1/2 teaspoon baking powder
- 1/2 teaspoon ground cinnamon
- 1/2 teaspoon chili powder
- 1/2 teaspoon kosher salt
- pinch cayenne pepper, optional
- 1/2 cup semi-sweet chocolate chips
- 1/2 cup milk chocolate chips
- Marshmallow Filling
- 1 cup marshmallow fluff
- 1/2 cup vegetable shortening
- 3/4 cup icing sugar
- 1 tablespoon whole milk
- 1/2 teaspoon vanilla extract

### Direction

- 1) Preheat oven to 350ºF. Line a baking sheet with parchment paper.
- 2) In a microwave safe bowl, melt semi-sweet chocolate and butter until smooth. In a large bowl, whisk sugar, eggs and vanilla. Whisk in melted chocolate mixture. Stir in flour, baking powder, cinnamon, chili powder, salt, cayenne pepper (if using) and both semi-sweet and milk chocolate chips, just until flour disappears. Drop the dough by tablespoon onto prepared baking sheet, at least 2 inches apart. Bake 9 minutes, or until the cookies are set. Remove from oven and cool before filling.
- 3) For the marshmallow filling, using an electric mixer, beat the marshmallow fluff and shortening until smooth. Add the icing sugar, milk and vanilla extract, beating for 1 minute until fluffy. Spread filling on the bottom of a cookie and top with another cookie.

## 55. Meyer Lemon Italian Ice Tiramisu Tart

*Serving: Serves 8-12 | Prep: | Cook: | Ready in:*

### Ingredients

- 1 tart crust
- 4 Meyer Lemons, zested and juiced
- 1 1/2 cups Mascarpone cheese
- 3/4 cup fresh whipped cream
- 2/3 cup lemon curd
- 2/3 cup marshmallow cream
- 2 Meyer Lemons, zested
- 2 tablespoons Italian Ice Syrup
- 2 teaspoons Lemoncello (optional)
- 5 lady fingers, crushed and sprinkled for garnish

### Direction

- 1 tart crust baked and ready to fill.
- For the Italian Ice Syrup: Bring to a boil the 4 lemons that were zested and juiced. Once it boils, take off heat, strain and allow to cool. Reserve 2 tablespoons of the syrup for the filling.
- In a bowl, mix the mascarpone cheese, lemon curd, marshmallow cream, 2 teaspoon of lemon zest, Italian ice syrup and lemon cello.

Fold in the whipped cream. Fill tart crust. Garnish crushed lady fingers and fresh Meyer Lemon zest. Optional: Add drunken raspberries for garnish that have been soaked in lemon cello.

## 56. Mimi's Sweet Potato Casserole

*Serving: Serves 5 to 6 | Prep: | Cook: | Ready in:*

### Ingredients

- 5 to 6  medium sweet potatoes
- Salt
- Dash of cinnamon
- Chopped nutes (almonds or walnuts)
- Butter for greasing
- Mini marshmallows, to top

### Direction

- Cook sweet potatoes in their jackets in a pot of boiling water until fork-tender. Drain and allow to cool for about 5 minutes for easy handling.
- Peal and mash well or whip lightly with a batter. Add salt and butter to taste. Add the chopped nuts and mix well.
- Lightly spoon the mixture into a buttered casserole and bake in moderately hot oven until well heated through. Remove from the oven and quickly top with miniature marshmallows for a decorative touch and return to the oven until marshmallows are delicately browned.

## 57. Mint Chocolate Rice Krispies Treats

*Serving: Serves 15 to 20, depending on how big you cut them | Prep: | Cook: | Ready in:*

### Ingredients

- 3 tablespoons  butter
- 1  10-ounce bag marshmallows
- 6 cups  crispy rice cereal
- 3/4 cup  miniature chocolate chips - OR -
- 1/2 cup  regular chocolate chips
- 1/3 to 1/2 cups  crushed hard peppermint candies

### Direction

- Melt butter in a large saucepan over low heat. Add marshmallows and cook, stirring, until completely melted.
- Take pan off heat. Stir in rice cereal. Gently fold in chocolate chips and peppermint candies. It's OK if the chips melt...it's part of what makes it good.
- Spread mixture in a 9x13-inch baking pan, or any high-sided baking pan. The size of the pan dictates how thick your treats will be.
- Set aside to cool and harden, about 30 minutes or so. Cover tightly, and keep at room temperature for up to 3 days...if they last that long!

## 58. Mississippi Mud Chocolate Cheesecake

*Serving: Serves 10 | Prep: | Cook: | Ready in:*

### Ingredients

- 24  chocolate wafer cookies
- 1/4 cup  melted butter
- 1 tablespoon  sugar
- 8 ounces  softened cream cheese
- 9.7 ounces  bar of chopped Bittersweet Chocolate
- 1/4 cup  cocoa powder,unsweetened
- 2 teaspoons  instant coffee granules
- 4  large egg
- 1/4 cup  sugar
- 1 teaspoon  vanilla extract

- 1/2 cup  cup pecans, chopped
- 6 ounces  chopped Bittersweet Chocolate
- 2 tablespoons  milk
- 1 tablespoon  sugar
- 1/2 cup  marshmallow cream
- 1/4 cup  pecans, chopped
- Bittersweet chocolate curls

## Direction

- For Crust-Preheat the oven to 350 degrees F or 175 degrees C. Grease a 3-inch by 9-inch springform pan with butter. Blend cookies, coffee granules and sugar in a processor and add melted butter until the ingredients blend properly. Spread the prepared mixture evenly onto bottom and not sides of prepared pan. Bake for 5 minutes and set aside to cool. Maintain oven temperature.
- For Filling-Melt the chopped bittersweet chocolate over a double boiler and stir occasionally until the chocolate melts. Cool the melted chocolate till it is lukewarm, but make sure it is still pourable. Now, add cocoa powder, instant coffee granules, cornstarch and sugar in a processor and blend, until smooth. Mix softened cream cheese and beat well till the cheese gets incorporated properly and all lumps disappear. Stir in the 4 eggs to it, one at a time, mixing slowly after each just until blended. Add vanilla extract with the last egg. Also add lukewarm chocolate and chopped pecans to this mixture and stir until it blends properly. Pour filling over the prepared crust and smoothen the top surface. Bake at 350 degrees F for 15 minutes, and then reduce the temperature to 200 degrees F and bake for another 2 hours. Cool for 5 minutes. Run knife around the rim of pan to loosen cake and chill overnight.
- For Topping-Melt chocolate chips, sugar and milk in a saucepan over low heat, until smooth. Pour marshmallow cream on the center of the cheesecake, and then spread it evenly over the top. Drizzle a layer of the chocolate mixture on the marshmallow cream and garnish with bittersweet chocolate curls

and chopped pecans. Transfer cheesecake to platter and serve chilled!!

## 59. Mississippi Mud Chocolate Cheesecake Recipe

*Serving: Serves 10 | Prep: | Cook: | Ready in:*

### Ingredients

- For Crust & filling
- 24 pieces  Chocolate wafer cookies
- 1/4 cup  Melted butter
- 1 tablespoon  Sugar
- 8   Softened cream cheese
- 9.7 ounces  Bar of chopped Bittersweet Chocolate
- 1/4 cup  Cocoa powder, unsweetened
- 4 pieces  Large eggs
- 1/4  Sugar
- 3 tablespoons  Cornstarch
- 1/2 cup  Pecans, chopped
- For Topping
- 6 ounces  Chopped Bittersweet Chocolate
- 1 tablespoon  Sugar
- 1/2 cup  Marshmallow cream
- 5 pieces  Bittersweet chocolate curls

### Direction

- For Crust & filling
- For Crust: Preheat the oven to 350 degrees F or 175 degrees C.
- Grease a 3-inch by 9-inch springform pan with butter.
- Blend cookies, coffee granules and sugar in a processor and add melted butter until the ingredients blend properly.
- Spread the prepared mixture evenly onto bottom and not sides of prepared pan.
- Bake for 5 minutes and set aside to cool. Maintain oven temperature.
- For Filling: Melt the chopped bittersweet chocolate over a double boiler and stir occasionally until the chocolate melts.

- Stir in the 4 eggs to it, one at a time, mixing slowly after each just until blended. Add vanilla extract with the last egg.
- Pour filling over the prepared crust and smoothen the top surface.
- Cool for 5 minutes. Run knife around the rim of pan to loosen cake and chill overnight.
- For Topping
- Melt chocolate chips, sugar and milk in a saucepan over low heat, until smooth.
- Pour marshmallow cream on the center of the cheesecake, and then spread it evenly over the top.

## 60. Modjeskas

*Serving: Makes about 15 candies | Prep: | Cook: | Ready in:*

### Ingredients

- 1 cup sugar
- 1/2 cup light corn syrup
- 1 cup heavy whipping cream
- 2 tablespoons unsalted butter
- 1/2 teaspoon salt
- 1 teaspoon vanilla extract
- Vanilla marshmallows, store-bought or homemade: https://food52.com/recipes...

### Direction

- Generously grease a marble slab or baking sheet and set aside. If using homemade marshmallows, cut into 1-inch squares. If using store-bought marshmallows, slice in half crosswise.
- In a heavy-bottom pot with a candy thermometer attached, combine sugar, syrup, and 1/2 cup of cream over medium-high heat. Bring to a boil, stirring continuously. Pour remaining 1/2 cup of cream into a small saucepan and warm (but do not boil) separately over low heat. Once the sugar mixture begins to boil, add the remaining warmed cream in a slow, steady stream. Add butter a half a tablespoon at a time, stirring until combined, and reduce heat to medium-low. Allow the mixture to boil until the temperature reaches 238°F, "soft ball" stage.
- Remove the mixture from the heat and stir in salt and vanilla extract. Allow to cool for about 5 minutes, and in that time, grab your greased baking sheet or slab. Using a fork, dip the marshmallows in the caramel until completely coated on all sides, then place on the greased baking sheet. Repeat to your heart's content. Allow candies to rest for 2 to 3 hours until fully set, then wrap individually using wax paper. Store in a cool, dry place.

## 61. New Zealand Lolly Cake

*Serving: Makes 20-25 slices | Prep: 2hours10mins | Cook: 0hours0mins | Ready in:*

### Ingredients

- 250 grams (about 20) digestive cookies or malt biscuits (if you can find them)
- 1/2 cup unsalted butter
- 1/2 cup sweetened condensed milk
- 1 1/2 cups multi-colored mini marshmallows (or regular if you can't find the colored kind)
- 1/2 cup desiccated coconut

### Direction

- Place cookies into a food processor and blitz into a fine crumb. If you don't have a food processor, place the cookies in a zip-top bag and bash them with a rolling pin into crumbs.
- In a small pot combine butter and sweetened condensed milk over low heat. Once butter has melted, mix well to combine and remove from heat.
- In a small bowl combine blitzed cookie crumbs and mini marshmallows. Pour melted butter and condensed milk mixture into bowl. Mix all ingredients together until well combined. Tip

mixture out onto a clean counter top and shape into a log that is about 3-inches in diameter. Roll the outsides of the log in the coconut. Wrap tightly in plastic wrap and place in the fridge to set (about 2-3 hours). You may need to re-roll log after 1 hour to re-set the log shape.
- Slice chilled log into ½ pieces. Serve. Keep leftovers in the fridge.

## 62. Nutella S'Mores

*Serving: Serves 4 | Prep: | Cook: | Ready in:*

### Ingredients

- 4 graham cracker sheets
- 4 tablespoons Nutella
- 4 handfuls mini marshmallows

### Direction

- Break your graham cracker sheets in half so you have 8 graham squares.
- Spread 1 Tablespoon of Nutella onto 4 of the 8 squares.
- Add a handful of mini marshmallows on top of each Nutella-filled square.
- Run a small pastry torch over the marshmallows to toast them. You could also place them under the broiler for a few seconds but be sure to keep an eye on them so they do not burn.
- Layer the other graham sheet on top of the toasted marshmallows.

## 63. Passover Rocky Road

*Serving: Makes 20 pieces | Prep: | Cook: | Ready in:*

### Ingredients

- 10 regular-size marshmallows (70 grams)
- 2 sheets matzo (I use the extra-thin and crispy kind), broken into bite-sized pieces
- Generous 1/2 cup walnut pieces (55 grams)
- 8 ounces milk or dark chocolate (up to about 64% cacao), coarsely chopped (225 grams)
- 1/8 teaspoon flaky sea salt, such as fleur de sel or Maldon

### Direction

- Line a baking sheet with parchment or wax paper.
- Cut each marshmallow in 6 pieces and toss them in a bowl with the matzo pieces and walnuts.
- Put the chocolate in a medium stainless bowl and set it directly in a wide skillet of almost simmering water. Stir until the chocolate is melted and smooth. Remove the bowl from the water and let the chocolate cool, stirring thoroughly and frequently, until it is at 90° F. Pour the matzo mixture over the chocolate and fold until the pieces are thoroughly coated -- there will be just enough chocolate. Use a spoon or your fingers to drop clusters on the parchment paper, or spread all of the mixture in a large layer. Sprinkle very tiny pinches of salt (crushing the largest flakes) over the chocolate.
- Refrigerate the pan for 10 to 15 minutes to set the chocolate. Serve at room temperature. Cut the sheet into squares or random pieces with a sharp knife, or break them apart with your hands.

## 64. Peanut Butter Banana S'more Sliders

*Serving: Serves 15 | Prep: | Cook: | Ready in:*

### Ingredients

- 1/2 loaf crusty artisan bread, sliced thin
- 4 tablespoons unsalted butter, room temperature

- 1 cup crunchy peanut butter
- 3 bananas, sliced
- 2 cups marshmallows, any variety
- 1/2 cup melted coconut oil
- 1/3 cup carob or cocoa powder

## Direction

- Preheat oven to 400 degrees F. spread butter on one side of each piece of bread. Place half the pieces of bread buttered side down on a foil lined baking sheet. Spread peanut butter on top and then top with bananas and marshmallows.
- Stir together the coconut oil and carob or cocoa powder until a syrup if formed. You may need more oil or powder depending on the consistency. It should pour like pancake syrup. Drizzle over the sliders. Top with another slice of bread, butter side up.
- Bake for about 20 minutes until marshmallows have melted and bread is toasty. Serve immediately or store at room temperature in an airtight container for up to 2 days.

## 65. Peanut Butter Cheerio Bars With M&M's

*Serving: Makes 9 large bars | Prep: | Cook: | Ready in:*

## Ingredients

- 1 tablespoon salted or unsalted butter (add a pinch of salt if you use unsalted)
- 10 ounces marshmallows
- 1 cup smooth peanut butter
- 6 cups Cheerio's
- 1 cup plain M&M's

## Direction

- Butter inside of 8 x 8 pan and set aside. Melt tablespoon butter in a large saucepan then add marshmallows and stir until melted. Add peanut butter and stir until blended. Add Cheerios and stir as gently and thoroughly as you can. I ended up dumping them into a bowl and using my clean hands. Add M&M's and carefully incorporate (many will break, but the color and flavor will be there and you can save a few to put on the top for presentation). Press into prepared pan (using a piece of wax paper will make this sticky job easier) and cool completely before cutting.

## 66. Peanut Butter Clusters

*Serving: Makes appx 48 | Prep: | Cook: | Ready in:*

## Ingredients

- 16 squares - White Almond Bark
- 1 cup Creamy Peanut Butter
- 2 cups Party or Cocktail Peanuts (no shells or husks)
- 3 cups Rice Krispies Cereal
- 2 cups Mini Marshmallows

## Direction

- Melt almond bark slowly in double boiler
- Once melted, stir in peanut butter to melt and combine well; then let cool slightly
- In separate, large bowl, combine peanuts, Rice Krispies and marshmallows
- Pour melted mixture over other ingredients in bowl and combine well
- Once combined, use a small cookie portion scoop (2 tsp size) to dip out + place on waxed paper to set up
- Once set, portion cookies into zip tight bags
- Clusters can be kept in refrigerator or freezer for long periods of time, as nothing will spoil
- If you make these during summer, keep them in the refrigerator or in a cooler (if at an outdoor function). They will 'slide' in warm weather and you might be eating them with a spoon!

## 67. Peanut Butter And Jelly Crispy Brown Rice Bars

*Serving: Makes 18-20 bars | Prep: | Cook: | Ready in:*

### Ingredients

- 4 tablespoons unsalted butter
- 10 ounces marshmallows
- 1 cup peanut butter
- 1 teaspoon vanilla extract
- 6 cups brown puffed rice cereal
- 1/2 cup raspberry preserves
- 1 teaspoon vanilla sea salt (or your favorite finishing salt)

### Direction

- In a deep saucepan over medium heat, add the butter. Once melted stir in the marshmallows and stir with a wooden spoon until melted. Add the peanut butter and vanilla, remove from heat, and stir to combine. Stir in the puffed brown rice cereal and make sure all pieces are evenly coated.
- Spoon half of the mixture into a greased 9×9-inch pan and press down with parchment to create an even, flat base. Pour the jam on top and spread an even layer across. Spoon the other half of the peanut butter and crispy rice mixture on top of the jam and push down with the parchment until evenly flat. Place in the refrigerator to cool completely, about 35 minutes. Cut into pieces and serve. Makes 18-20 bars, depending on how large you would like them.

## 68. Peanut Butter Cereal Treats

*Serving: Makes a 9x13" pan of treats | Prep: | Cook: | Ready in:*

### Ingredients

- 4 tablespoons coconut oil
- 1 cup Cracklin' Oat Bran, smashed up a bit
- 2 cups Honey Bunches of Oats
- 1 Brown Rice Crispies (regular ones are okay too)
- 2 cups Corn Chex
- 8 ounces Reese's pieces
- 2 Butterfinger fun-sized bars, smashed up into small pieces
- 1 bag mini-marshmallows
- 1 cup chunky peanut butter
- 2 pinches salt

### Direction

- Coat a 9x13" dish with 1 tablespoon of the coconut oil
- Mix all of the cereals and mix-ins in a large bowl
- Melt the remaining coconut oil over medium heat. Once melted, add the marshmallows and reduce the heat to low until completely melted. Add in the peanut butter and salt and stir until smooth and creamy.
- If your pot is large enough, dump your cereal and mix-ins into it and stir quickly to coat. Otherwise, pour your hot marshmallow-peanut butter mixture into the bowl with the cereal and work quickly to coat. As soon as you have evenly mixed your ingredients, get them into the oiled pan. Cover with aluminum foil/wax paper/saran wrap (whichever you have around) and press down firmly to form the treats together. Let cool (if you can!), then cut and serve.

## 69. Peppermint Marshmallow Hot Chocolate Cookies

*Serving: Makes 24 cookies | Prep: | Cook: | Ready in:*

### Ingredients

- For The Cookies:
- 1 3/4 cups all-purpose flour

- 3/4 cup cocoa powder
- 1/2 teaspoon baking soda
- 1/2 teaspoon salt
- 1/2 cup unsalted butter, softened (1 stick)
- 1 cup sugar
- 1 large egg
- 1/2 cup almond milk (or regular milk)
- 1 teaspoon peppermint extract
- 1 teaspoon vanilla extract
- 10 ounces mini-marshmallows
- 8 mini candy canes gently broken into small pieces (or use 4 large candy canes)
- For The Chocolate Ganache Drizzle:
- 3/8 cup heavy whipping cream
- 5 ounces semi-sweet chocolate morsels

## Direction

- Unwrap candy canes (if they are wrapped) and place them in a freezer-weight resealable bag. Using the flat side of a kitchen mallet or meat tenderizer, gently tap on the canes to break them into small pieces (do not over-do this or you will end up with only peppermint dust!). Separate the pieces from the dust, and set aside.
- Preheat oven to 375 degrees. In a medium bowl, whisk together flour, cocoa powder, baking soda, and salt. Set aside.
- Use an electric mixer to cream together butter and sugar until light and fluffy, about 2-3 minutes. Add egg, milk, vanilla, and peppermint extract, then beat until well combined. Add the flour and other dry ingredients from the first bowl a little at a time, and mix on low speed until combined.
- Using a 2-tablespoon scoop, drop dough onto parchment-lined baking sheet. Arrange cookies evenly with plenty of room between them. Bake until they start to spread and become firm, 10 minutes.
- Remove from oven, place four mini-marshmallows in the center of each cookie, and bake another 2 minutes, or until the marshmallows begin to melt. Transfer cookies to a wire rack to cool completely.
- While the cookies are cooling, make the chocolate ganache drizzle: place semi-sweet chocolate chips in a heat-proof mixing bowl. Heat the heavy cream in a small saucepan until it is almost simmering, then pour it over the chocolate chips. Wait 3 minutes then whisk thoroughly and then allow the ganache to rest for about 5 minutes.
- Using a fork, carefully drizzle the chocolate ganache across each cookie, leaving some of the marshmallow exposed. Test the ganache on a side plate to make sure it is ready, and if it's too thin, allow it to cool further before using.
- Top each cookie with the candy cane pieces and enjoy!

## 70. Peppermint Rice Krispies Treats

*Serving: Serves 18 | Prep: | Cook: | Ready in:*

## Ingredients

- 1 cup white chocolate peppermint covered pretzels, chopped
- 1 cup soft peppermint candies, chopped (like Andes)
- 4 cups peppermint mini marshmallows
- 2 cups regular mini marshmallows
- 3 tablespoons unsalted butter, cubed
- 4 cups Rice Krispies
- 1/2 cup soft peppermint candies, melted, for drizzling (like Andes)

## Direction

- Line a 9 by 13 inch pan with parchment. Set aside.
- Coarsely chop pretzels and candies. I cut the pretzels into quarters and the candies into thirds. Measure prior to chopping. Set aside. Measure out Rice Krispies and set aside.
- In a large microwave safe bowl, microwave both kinds of marshmallows and butter in 30 second increments, stirring in between to

promote melting, until they are completely melted. Immediately pour in pretzels, candies, and Rice Krispies. Stir until all ingredients are evenly distributed and fully coated with marshmallow. Quickly pour the mixture into the prepared pan, smoothing down with hands.

- In a small microwave safe bowl, melt the Andes chips in 30 second increments, stirring in between to promote melting, until fully melted. Immediately drizzle over the pan of treats.
- Allow treats to cool completely in the pan before cutting into squares and serving. May be stored at room temperature in an airtight container for up to 3 days, though they are best the first day.

## 71. Popcorn Toasted Cereal Cake

*Serving: Makes a bundt tin | Prep: | Cook: | Ready in:*

### Ingredients

- 10 cups of freshly popped corn ( I made mine using about 1/2 cup of corn kernels)
- 1/4 cup unsalted butter, melted
- Pinch of salt
- 1 scant cup granola (or crunchy, toasted cereal of your choice)
- 1 cup white chocolate chips (1/2 cup to make the marshmallow sauce, and 1/2 to toss with the popcorn)
- 3/4 scant cup M&Ms ( regular or peanut, up to you)
- 1/2 cup broken (not crushed/ground) crispy pretzel sticks
- 1 cup mini marshmallows
- 1/4 cup unsalted butter, room temperature

### Direction

- Prepare a 10" tube or Bundt pan by spraying with cooking spray. (You can use a large pan but your cake won't be as high. It won't affect the deliciousness though...) Place the freshly popped corn in a large, wide bowl, being careful to remove the un-popped kernels. To jazz up plain popcorn, drizzle 1/4 cup of melted butter over the popcorn, add a pinch of salt and toss well to combine. Let cool completely, about 5 - 10 minutes.
- Add the cereal, M&M, broken pretzel sticks and 1/2 cup of white chocolate chips to the popcorn. Toss and set aside while you prepare the 'sauce' which will make it a cake.
- In a large saucepan, melt the 1/4 cup of room temperature butter, over low heat. Add the mini marshmallows and the remaining 1/2 cup white chocolate chips. Stir until melted and smooth - a few minutes. Be careful not to turn your back on the sauce as it so easily burns.
- Remove from heat, let the sauce cool down for about 5 minutes before pouring it over your popcorn-cereal mix. Too soon and the heat will cause the popcorn to shrink into nothingness - not very pleasant! Stir all the ingredients together till combined, then fill the pan and press in.
- Cover with foil and let the popcorn cake set for at least an hour, up to 4 hours.
- Once set, gently run a table/butter knife round the rim. Invert your pan over a serving platter et voila, your cake is here. Beautiful, and totally delicious. Cover tightly and store for up to 1 day. Ours didn't last an hour. Every grain that was left, was eaten off the table and off the platter.

## 72. Pumpkin Marshmallow Toffee Cookies

*Serving: Makes 18 | Prep: | Cook: | Ready in:*

### Ingredients

- 1/2 cup (1 Stick) Unsalted Butte
- 1/4 cup Packed Light Brown Sugar

- 1/2 cup  Granulated Sugar
- 6 tablespoons  Pumpkin Puree (Not pumpkin filling)
- 1 and 1/2 cups  All-Purpose Flour
- 1/4 teaspoon  Salt
- 1/4 teaspoon  Baking Powder
- 1/4 teaspoon  Baking Soda
- 1 and 1/2 teaspoons  Ground Cinnamon
- 1/4 teaspoon  Ground Nutmeg
- 1/4 teaspoon  Ground Cloves
- 1/4 teaspoon  Allspice
- 1/2 cup  Mini Semi-Sweet Chocolate Chips
- 1/2 cup  Toffee Chips
- 1/2 cup  Mini Marshmallows, cut in half

## Direction

- In a medium bowl, whisk the melted butter, brown sugar, and granulated sugar together until no lumps remain. Whisk in the vanilla and pumpkin puree until smooth. Set aside.
- In a large bowl, toss together the flour, salt, baking powder, baking soda, cinnamon, nutmeg, allspice, and cloves. Pour the wet ingredients into the dry ingredients and mix together with a large spoon or rubber spatula. Fold in ½ cup mini semi-sweet chocolate chips and ½ cup toffee chips until evenly dispersed in the dough. Cover the dough and chill for at least 30 minutes.
- Roll the dough into balls, about 1.5 Tablespoons of dough each and slightly flatten with the palm of your hand.
- Bake the cookies for 7 minutes. Remove from the oven and press 3-4 pieces of marshmallow halves on top of each cookie. Return to the oven for another 2-3 minutes. Remove from the oven. Cookies will appear undone and very soft. Press a few more chocolate chips or toffee pieces onto the tops, if desired.
- Allow the cookies to cool for at least 10 minutes on the cookie sheets before transferring to a wire rack to cool completely, about 1 hour.
- Store in an air-tight container at room temperature for up to seven days.

# 73. Pumpkin Spie Latte Macaron Cookies

*Serving: Serves 12 | Prep:  | Cook:  | Ready in:*

## Ingredients

- Macaron Shell
- 42 grams  almond flour
- 50 grams  powdered sugar
- 4 grams  pumpkin pie spice
- 4 grams  finely ground coffee
- 40 grams  egg whites
- 40 grams  granulated sugar
- Filling
- 1/2 cup  marshmallow fluff
- 1/2 cup  pumpkin pie spice
- 1 cup  marshmallow fluff
- 1/2 cup  softened butter
- 1 tablespoon  pumpkin puree
- 1 teaspoon  pumpkin pie spice
- 1 teaspoon  instant expresso powder

## Direction

- Macaroon Shells: 1. in a food processor, grind together the almond flour, powder sugar, pumpkin pie spice, and coffee grounds
- 2. Sive the dry ingredients through a fine mesh strainer into a bowl. Set aside
- 3. in a separate bowl, whip the egg whites till foamy
- 4. Gradually add in the granulated sugar, then whip till stiff peaks form
- 5. In three portions, add the dry ingredients into the egg whites. Fold the dry ingredients into the egg whites carefully, but not too gently (this will cause too many big air pockets and make the shells crack).
- 6. Keep folding the mixture until it flows off the spatula like lava in a thick ribbon.
- 7. Transfer the mixture to a piping bag with a tip.
- 8. Pipe 2-inch circles onto a tray lined with silpat (using a template helps a lot).

- 9. Once you've piped all your batter, tap the tray on the counter until the macaroons smooth out. Pop any bubbles that form with a toothpick.
- 10. Preheat the oven to 300 degrees F and let the macaroons rest while the oven pre-heats.
- 11. Bake the macaroons for 7 minutes then rotate and bake for another 7 minutes
- Filling: 1. mix the 1/2 cup marshmallow fluff with the pumpkin pie spice, place in a piping bag with a star tip and set aside. 2. Whip the softened butter on high until it turns pale ivory in color. 3. Combine the pumpkin pie puree with the instant espresso powder and pumpkin pie spice. 4. Add the pumpkin mixture to the butter and whip till combined. 5. Add the cup of marshmallow fluff to the butter mixture and whip till combined. 6. Place the buttercream into a piping bag with a round tip.
- Assemble: 1. Match up the macaroon shells. 2. Pipe the spiced marshmallow fluff in a ring on one of the shells. 3. Fill the ring with the pumpkin espresso buttercream 4. Sandwich the two shells together. 5. Use a blowtorch to torch the outer ring of marshmallow fluff. 6. Enjoy!

## 74. Pumpkin Whoopie Pies With Maple Cream Filling

*Serving: Serves about two dozen | Prep: | Cook: | Ready in:*

## Ingredients

- Filling
- 1 cup powdered sugar, sifted
- 1 cup unsalted butter, room temperature
- 1 7-oz. jar marshmallow creme
- 2 teaspoons maple extract
- Cake
- 3 cups all-purpose flour
- 2 teaspoons ground cinammon
- 1 1/2 teaspoons baking powder
- 1 1/2 teaspoons baking soda
- 3/4 teaspoon salt
- 3/4 teaspoon ground nutmeg
- 3/4 teaspoon ground cloves
- 6 tablespoons unsalted butter, room temperature
- 3/4 cup packed golden brown sugar
- 3/4 cup sugar
- 1/2 cup vegetable oil
- 3 large eggs
- 1 15-oz. can pure pumpkin
- 1/2 cup milk
- non-stick vegetable oil spray

## Direction

- To make the filling, beat sugar and butter in large bowl in an electric mixer until fluffy, about 2 minutes. Add marshmallow crème and maple extract; beat until blended and smooth. Set aside.
- Sift first 7 ingredients into large bowl. Using electric mixer, beat butter and both sugars in another large bowl until blended. Gradually beat in oil. Add eggs 1 at a time, beating to blend between additions. Beat in pumpkin. Add dry ingredients in 2 additions alternately with milk in 1 addition, beating to blend between additions and occasionally scraping down sides of bowl. Cover and chill batter 1 hour.
- Arrange 1 rack in bottom third of oven and 1 rack in top third of oven; preheat to 350°F. Line 2 baking sheets with parchment; spray lightly with nonstick spray. Spoon batter onto baking sheet to form cakes (about 3 level tablespoons each; about 12 per baking sheet), spacing apart. Let stand 10 minutes.
- Bake cakes until tester inserted into centers comes out clean, about 20 minutes, rotating sheets halfway through baking. Cool cakes completely on baking sheets on rack. Using metal spatula, remove cakes from parchment.
- Line cooled baking sheets with clean parchment; spray with nonstick spray, and repeat baking with remaining batter.

- Spoon about 2 tablespoons filling on flat side of 1 cake. Top with another cake, flat side down. Repeat with remaining cakes and filling.

## 75. Quisp Cereal, Candied Bacon And Marshmallow Cookie

*Serving: Makes 15 cookies | Prep: | Cook: | Ready in:*

### Ingredients

- 2 1/2 cups  AP flour
- 1/2 teaspoon  Baking soda
- 7 ounces  Unsalted butter, room temperature
- 3/4 cup  Granulated sugar
- 1/2 cup  Dark brown sugar divided
- 2 cups  Quisp cereal
- 2 cups  Mini marshmallows
- i cups  Crispy bacon chopped finely in food processor
- 2  Large Eggs
- 2 teaspoons  Vanilla
- 1/2 teaspoon  Whiskey

### Direction

- In a small sauté pan, take crispy bacon and the 1/4 cup dark brown sugar and store to coat until all sugar is dissolved and bacon well coated. Set aside.
- In a large mixing bowl, cream the butter, granulated sugar and 1/4 dark brown sugar until fluffy. Add eggs, whiskey, vanilla and beat well. Add the bacon and marshmallows, mix to combine.
- In another bowl whisk flour, soda, and salt. Add dry mixture to mixing bowl and mix just until combined. Release the beater blade and gently stir in the Quisp cereal. It's okay if they crunch up a bit.
- Turn oven to 350 degrees. Line a sheet pan with parchment. The marshmallows with make a mess of your pans if you don't. I use a 1 1/2 tablespoon cookie scooper. Scoop cookies on sheet pan, no more than 12 per sheet. Before cookies go into oven I like to sprinkle a tiny bit of sea salt on the tops of each cookie! Gives it a nice sweet salty combo taste. I like my cookies underdone so I bake mine 8-10 minutes. Just until it is no longer raw but still very under done.

## 76. Red Velvet Milkshake

*Serving: Serves 1 | Prep: | Cook: | Ready in:*

### Ingredients

- 2 cups  vanilla ice cream
- 1/2 cup  red velvet cake mix
- 1/4 cup  whole milk
- 2 ounces  cream cheese
- 1/2 teaspoon  vanilla extract
- marshmallow fluff, to rim glass and garnish
- multi colored sprinkles, to rim glass

### Direction

- Place sprinkles on a large plate. Rub the rim of a tall milkshake glass with marshmallow fluff. Dip the glass in sprinkles and set aside.
- For the milkshake, using a blender, combine vanilla ice cream, red velvet cake mix, milk, cream cheese and vanilla extract. Blend until smooth and pour into prepared milkshake glass. Spoon marshmallow fluff over top of the milkshake to garnish.

## 77. Rice Crispies And Mixed Nut Balls

*Serving: Serves 3 people | Prep: | Cook: | Ready in:*

### Ingredients

- 1/2 cup  Marshmallows
- 4 cups  Rice crispies

- 1 cup  Dark Chocolate chips
- 2 tablespoons  Honey
- 2 tablespoons  milk
- 2 tablespoons  Water
- 1/4 cup  Almond powder
- 1/4 cup  Dried chopped nuts of your choice
- 1/4 cup  Butter or margarine

### Direction

- Add the marshmallows milk and water in a microwaveable bowl and MW for 1 min in high. The mash mallow melts. Stir well and MW again for 2 mins. The marshmallows should have melted by this time now to a softened jelly form.
- Grind coarsely the rice krispies and add the rice krispies, honey, almond powder to the softened marshmallow and mix well. When the mixture is lukewarm make balls with the mixture
- Place the butter in a bowl and MW for 2 mins in high and to the melted butter add the chocolate chips and stir well, you get a silky soft melted chocolate.
- Now coat the rice crispy balls with melted chocolate and sprinkle the chopped dried nuts over and keep it in fridge for an hour.
- Rice crispy balls are ready to serve now.
- This can be stored in a cool place for a month.
- Depending upon your microwave the time varies* this can be done without the microwave too by using the ordinary stove

## 78. Rocky Road

*Serving: Makes 3 pounds | Prep: | Cook: | Ready in:*

### Ingredients

- 8 ounces  (225 grams) regular large marshmallows, snipped in quarters
- 2 cups  (slightly generous, 225 grams) walnut halves (or large pieces)
- 2 pounds  (900 grams) dark, milk, or white chocolate (from wafers or pistoles or bars, but not chocolate chips) melted and either cooled to 90° F or tempered

### Direction

- Line a baking sheet with parchment paper. Use a large rubber or Silicone spatula to fold the snipped marshmallows and walnuts into the chocolate, turning the mixture over and over and scraping the chocolate from the bottom and sides of the bowl, until all of the pieces are coated with chocolate. Immediately scrape the mixture onto the parchment lined sheet, forming a long bumpy log shape about 3 1/2 to 4 inches wide and 20 to 22 inches long.
- If the chocolate was tempered, place the baking sheet it in a cool place, or in front of a fan (I keep an electric fan for just this purpose!) for at least 30 minutes to set the chocolate. If the chocolate was not tempered, set the pan in the fridge until the chocolate it set.
- When the chocolate is thoroughly set, use a sharp serrated knife to cut the log (crosswise or on the diagonal) into slices about 1/2-inch thick.
- Store rocky road in an airtight container in a cool place if the chocolate was tempered, or in the refrigerator if it was not.

## 79. Rocky Road Potato Chip Bites

*Serving: Makes a lot (see headnote) | Prep: 0hours10mins | Cook: 1hours0mins | Ready in:*

### Ingredients

- 9 ounces  semisweet chocolate chips (about 3/4 of an average bag)
- 1 1/2 cups  smooth peanut butter
- 3 cups  roughly crushed potato chips (I used Ruffles; don't go crazy crushing these! They

will inevitably crush more when you're stirring them into the melty chocolate mixture)
- 3 cups mini marshmallows

## Direction

- Do you want to enjoy these suckers in square or wedge form? You must make a choice. For squares, line a rimmed baking sheet with parchment paper. For wedges, line two pie tins or round cake pans instead.
- In a large pot over low heat, melt the chocolate and peanut butter together until smooth and shiny. Remove from the heat. With a heatproof spatula, fold in the chips and marshmallows until completely coated.
- If making squares, dump the chocolaty mess onto the sheet and spread into a single, flat layer with your spatula. For wedges, press this mess into the pie tins or cake pans.
- Stick the baking sheet or pie tins in the fridge for 2 hours or freezer for 1, until hardened. Pull them out and slice them up into squares or wedges.
- Store these guys in the fridge or freezer with the layers separated by parchment paper. I'm not gonna tell you that they're blow-your-mind awesome with a scoop of ice cream on top…but I'm also not NOT gonna tell you that either.

## 80. Rocky Road Toffee

*Serving: Makes 19 x 13 inch pan | Prep: | Cook: |Ready in:*

## Ingredients

- 4 ounces Orgran Toasted Buckwheat Crisp Bread (enough to line 9 X 13-inch pan)
- 8 ounces unsalted butter
- 3/4 cup brown sugar
- 1/4 cup almond butter (okay to substitute smooth peanut butter)
- 1 teaspoon vanilla extract
- 1/4 teaspoon sea salt
- 1/2 cup white marshmallows, chopped
- 1/2 cup sliced almonds
- 8 ounces dark chocolate, roughly chopped
- 1/2 cup hazelnuts, chopped

## Direction

- Preheat oven to 350 degrees.
- Fully line a 9 X 13-inch baking pan with parchment paper, up the sides, or with foil sprayed with non-sticky baking spray.
- Place the crackers in a single layer, completely covering the pan.
- Combine the butter, sugar, almond butter, vanilla and salt in a medium saucepan and gently bring to a boil. Whisk to dissolve the sugar. Reduce the heat and simmer 1 minute, constantly whisking.
- Pour the mixture over the crackers. Using an offset spatula, spread the mixture evenly.
- Bake 8-9 minutes. Remove from the oven, scatter half the chocolate, all the marshmallows, sliced almonds and top with remaining chocolate. Return to oven for approximately 1 minute to melt the chocolate.
- Remove from oven and sprinkle the chopped hazelnuts. Allow to cool completely.
- Use baking paper or foil to lift entire slab out of the pan. Using a sharp knife, cut into pieces; or if freezing, gently remove Toffee from paper and wrap in waxed paper and then plastic wrap.
- Place wrapped slab in airtight container and freeze.

## 81. Russian Bird`s Milk Cake Ice Cream

*Serving: Serves 4 | Prep: | Cook: |Ready in:*

## Ingredients

- 200 milliliters whole milk
- 200 milliliters heavy cream

- 130 grams sugar
- 1 pinch salt
- 3 teaspoons cornstarch
- 100 grams marshmallows
- 20 grams cocoa powder
- 30 grams dark chocolate
- 70 grams shortbread fingers

### Direction

- For the chocolate sauce in a small saucepan over medium heat combine 80ml water, 45gr sugar, the sifted cocoa powder, cook 2min stirring until uniform. Add the chopped dark chocolate, cook until completely melted and glossy.
- Dissolve the cornstarch in 50ml whole milk, leave to rest.
- For the ice cream base in a small saucepan over medium heat combine the leftover milk, heavy cream, 85gr sugar, a pinch of salt and 100gr Original Marshmallow Fluff or plain marshmallows and cook until fully dissolved. Add the cornstarch milk and cook constantly stirring until thickened and glossy smooth. Take off heat, cool to room temp and transfer into the fridge overnight.
- Freeze in your ice cream maker according to the manufacturer's instructions adding the crushed shortbread cookies at the last couple of minutes of churning. Store in an airtight container alternating layers of ice cream and the chocolate sauce and store in the freezer until set.

## 82. S'Mores Brownie Ice Cream Sandwiches

*Serving: Makes 24 sandwiches | Prep: | Cook: | Ready in:*

### Ingredients

- 4 cups mini marshmallows
- 14 ounces box of graham crackers
- 1 box family size brownie mix (for a 9"x13" pan), prepared for the chewy version
- 2 tablespoons butter, melted
- 2 cups whole milk
- 4 teaspoons vanilla extract
- 2 cups heavy cream

### Direction

- Turn the broiler on in your oven. Line a baking sheet with a Silpat, foil, or parchment paper. Spread the marshmallows out in a single layer. Broil the marshmallows for 1 minute or until nice and toasted. Remove from oven and chill in the freezer so that it is easier to remove from the baking sheet. Reduce the temperature in the oven to 350°F.
- In the meantime, carefully break the graham crackers into squares. Spread them out on the bottom of a 9"x13" pan and a 9"x9" pan to make sure you have enough to cover the surface area twice. You may have to break up some of the squares to make them fit. Remove the graham crackers and line the bottom of the two pans with parchment paper. Spray with cooking spray.
- Pour a little more than half the brownie batter into the larger pan and the rest into the smaller pan. You want to try to get the same thickness in both pans. Brush both sides of the graham crackers with the melted butter and cover the top of the brownie batter in both pans with half the crackers. Place the rest of the crackers onto another baking sheet.
- Put the two brownie pans on the middle rack of your oven and the sheet with the graham crackers on the lower rack. Bake for 10 minutes and start checking to see if the brownies are close to done. You want them to still be a little gooey (they will continue to cook once out of the oven and set upon cooling) but not raw and liquidy. Once the brownies are ready, remove all the pans and the sheet from the oven and allow to cool. After ten minutes, move the brownies to the freezer to chill for at least 30 minutes.

- While the brownies are chilling, place the toasted marshmallows in a medium pot and add the milk. Cook over medium-high, stirring regularly, until the marshmallows melt into the milk. Remove from heat, stir in vanilla extract and allow to cool. Chill until cold.
- Take the brownie-cracker pans out of the freezer. Lift and peel the parchment paper to remove it from the pan. Then, line the pan again with parchment paper and invert the brownie and cracker back into the pan so that now, the cracker-layer is facing down and lining the pan. If you have trimmed/uneven crackers, take note of which sides the uneven crackers are. You'll want to match the top and bottom layer so you can make even cuts later.
- When marshmallow mixture is cold, beat whipped cream to soft peaks and fold into the marshmallow base. Pour the ice cream batter on top of the brownie and smooth the top with a spoon. Arrange the crackers on top of the ice cream batter, making sure that the cracker arrangement matches the bottom cracker-layer (the uneven cracker pieces should be on the same side of the pan). Move the pan back into the freezer to harden, at least 8 hours to overnight.
- Cut between the crackers to make little sandwiches. Wrap each with plastic wrap and store in the freezer.

## 83. S'mores Bark

*Serving: Serves 4-6 | Prep: | Cook: |Ready in:*

## Ingredients

- 2 cups semi-sweet chocolate chips
- 1 cup white chocolate chips
- 3/4 cup graham crackers, broken into pieces
- 3/4 cup mini marshmallows
- 2 milk chocolate bars, broken into pieces

## Direction

- Place semi-sweet chocolate chips in a medium bowl. Microwave for 30 seconds and stir. Continue to microwave in 20 second intervals, stirring after each interval, until smooth.
- Place white chocolate chips in a medium bowl. Microwave for 30 seconds and stir. Continue to microwave in 20 second intervals, stirring after each interval, until smooth.
- Pour milk chocolate mixture on baking sheet lined with wax paper. Spoon white chocolate over top and use a toothpick or knife to swirl through. Sprinkle with graham cracker bits, mini marshmallows and broke pieces of milk chocolate bars. Place in freezer for 1-2 hours. When ready to serve, break into pieces and enjoy!

## 84. S'mores Brownies

*Serving: Serves 20 | Prep: | Cook: |Ready in:*

## Ingredients

- For the crust:
- 1 cup Graham cracker crumbs
- 1/4 cup Melted butter
- 1/4 cup Brown sugar
- for the brownies:
- 1/2 cup Butter
- 1 cup Sugar
- 1 teaspoon Vanilla extract
- 2 eggs
- 1/2 cup Unbleached all purpose flour
- 1/3 cup Unsweetened cocoa powder
- 1/4 teaspoon baking powder
- 1/4 teaspoon Salt
- 1/4 cup Small marshmallows
- 2 tablespoons marshmellow fluff

## Direction

- Preheat oven to 350 degrees F.
- Grease a 9x9 inch baking pan with shortening.

- Crush graham crackers into crumbs, then mix with melted butter and brown sugar and press into the bottom of the pan.
- In a medium bowl, mix together the butter, sugar, and vanilla.
- Mix in eggs.
- Combine flour, cocoa, baking powder, and salt in a small bowl; gradually stir into the egg and sugar mixture until well blended.
- Spread the batter evenly into the baking pan.
- Spoon marshmallow fluff over the top, then use a knife to swirl in to the batter. Top with small marshmallows.
- Bake for 20 to 25 minutes. Remove from oven once center is cooked and edges are pulling away from pan.

## 85. S'mores Cheesecake

*Serving: Makes 3 4-inch cheesecakes | Prep: | Cook: | Ready in:*

### Ingredients

- 3/4 cup  graham cracker crumbs
- 3 tablespoons  butter, melted
- 2 tablespoons  sugar
- 6 tablespoons  chocolate chips
- 2  eggs
- 1 cup  marshmallow fluff
- 2 teaspoons  vanilla extract
- 1/4 cup  dark chocolate chips
- 1/4 cup  heavy whipping cream
- mini marshmallows

### Direction

- Grease three 4-inch cheesecakes pans and set aside. Preheat oven to 350°F.
- In a small bowl, combine graham cracker crumbs, melted butter and sugar. Stir to combine. Equally divide between the three cheesecake pans and press them into the bottom. Place in the oven and bake for 7-8 minutes, until fragrant. After you remove the pans from the oven, sprinkle each crust with 2 tablespoons of chocolate chips. Reduce heat to 325°F.
- In the bowl of a stand mixer, combine softened cream cheese and sugar until light and fluffy with no clumps. Add eggs one at a time and mix well to incorporate. Add vanilla and 1 cup marshmallow fluff and mix again until incorporated. Divide the cheesecake evenly between the three pans and place in the oven. Bake for 35-40 minutes, until set in the middle. Remove from the oven and allow to cool completely. Cover with plastic wrap and place in refrigerator for at least two hours.
- To make the chocolate ganache, add chocolate and cream to a double boiler and stir until the chocolate is melted and the cream is no longer visible. Remove from heat and spread over cheesecakes.
- Right before serving, add marshmallows to the top of the cheesecakes and use a hand held kitchen torch to toast them. If you don't have a torch, spread the marshmallows on a parchment lined baking sheet and put under the broiler in your oven for 30 seconds to a minute, watching them very closely. Scoop them off of the baking sheet and onto the cheesecakes. Top with graham cracker crumbs and a drizzle of chocolate.

## 86. S'mores Chocolate Tart

*Serving: Makes 1 9-inch tart | Prep: | Cook: | Ready in:*

### Ingredients

- Graham Cracker Crust
- 1 3/4 cups  graham cracker crumbs
- 1/2 cup  unsalted butter, melted
- 1/4 cup  granulated sugar
- Tart
- 1 cup  marshmallow fluff
- 130 grams  dark chocolate, chopped
- 130 grams  milk chocolate, chopped
- 260 milliliters  heavy cream

- 1/2 cup mini marshmallows (optional)

## Direction

- Graham Cracker Crust
- Pre-heat oven to 350 F
- Mix together graham cracker crumbs, butter and sugar until it feels like wet sand. Using the bottom of a cup, press the mixture into the pan and onto the edges. The edges should be at least 1 inch high. Make sure you pack it nice and tight.
- Tart
- Pop the marshmallow fluff into the microwave for 10 seconds so it's easy to spread. Using an offset spatula, gently spread the fluff onto the crust.
- You can brown the marshmallow fluff two ways! 1) Set the crust under a broiler and watch it carefully to make sure the crust doesn't burn. 2) Use a crème brulee torch to caramelize the fluff. Set the crust aside
- Add chopped chocolate to medium sized bowl. In a heavy bottom saucepan, bring heavy cream to a boil while stirring constantly. Pour the hot heavy cream over the chocolate. Let this sit for 3 minutes.
- Stir the heavy cream and chocolate together until you get a silky smooth ganache.
- Pour the ganache into the crust. Tap the pan onto a table to get rid of any air bubbles. Sprinkle mini marshmallows on top for decoration.
- Refrigerate overnight and enjoy!

## 87. S'mores Cookies

*Serving: Makes 24 cookies | Prep: | Cook: | Ready in:*

## Ingredients

- 1 cup miniature marshmallows
- 1 cup all-purpose flour
- 1 cup finely crushed graham cracker crumbs
- 1/2 cup cocoa powder (I like dark or black cocoa powder for these)
- 1 teaspoon baking powder
- 1/2 teaspoon salt
- 1/2 cup butter, softened
- 1/2 cup granulated sugar
- 1/2 cup brown sugar
- 2 eggs
- 1 teaspoon vanilla extract
- 1 1/2 cups dark chocolate chunks or chips
- 1/2 cup shredded unsweetened coconut

## Direction

- Put the marshmallows in an uncovered bowl and leave them out at room temperature overnight. "Aging" the marshmallows encourages them to keep their shape while baking.
- In a large bowl, whisk together the flour, graham cracker crumbs, cocoa, baking powder, and salt. Set aside.
- In a large bowl or stand mixer, cream the butter and sugars until very light.
- Add the eggs and vanilla and beat until fluffy (at least 3 minutes).
- Slowly add the flour mixture, stopping to scrape down the sides of the bowl. Stop mixing once the dough is fully blended and don't over mix.
- Stir in the chocolate chunks, coconut, and marshmallows and mix evenly.
- Chill the dough for at least 1 hour before baking.
- When you're ready to bake, preheat the oven to 350° F.
- Spoon heaping tablespoonfuls of dough onto parchment-lined baking sheets, leaving room for spreading, and bake for 12 to 15 minutes (depending on the size of your cookie, it will take more or less time). The cookies should be set on the outsides but still soft in the middle.
- Let the cookies cool on the sheet for at least 5 minutes, then transfer them to a wire rack to finish cooling.

# 88. S'mores Croissants

*Serving: Makes 18 croissants | Prep: | Cook: | Ready in:*

## Ingredients

- For the graham puff pastry:
- 2 1/2 teaspoons active dry yeast
- 1 1/4 cups warm milk
- 1 cup graham flour
- 1 1/2 cups plus 2 tablespoons all-purpose flour, divided, plus more as needed
- 1 tablespoon wheat gluten flour
- 1/4 cup dark brown sugar
- 1/2 teaspoon cinnamon
- 1 teaspoon salt
- 25 tablespoons (3 sticks, plus 1 tablespoon) unsalted butter, divided
- For the croissants and assembly:
- 9 ounces (about 6 standard Hershey bars) milk chocolate
- 12 ounces mini marshmallows
- 1 egg, beaten

## Direction

- For the graham puff pastry:
- First, make the dough: In the bowl of a stand mixer, combine the yeast and warm milk and set aside.
- In a large bowl, combine the flours, brown sugar, and cinnamon. Whisk together. Check to make sure that the yeast is foamy, then add the dry ingredients to the stand mixer.
- Using a dough hook, knead the dough on low speed until a ball forms, about 3 minutes. Add 1 tablespoon of butter and continue to knead until the dough is smooth and pliable but not sticky, about 5 minutes. (You may need to add a few more tablespoons of flour if the dough is too sticky.) Wrap the dough in plastic wrap and refrigerate.
- In the bowl of the stand mixer (no need to put too much effort into washing it), combine 2 tablespoons of flour and the remaining 24 tablespoons of butter. Beat on medium-high speed with a paddle attachment until the butter is smooth and pliable.
- Roll out a sheet of plastic wrap (about 14 inches long). Using a rubber spatula, scrape the butter mixture directly onto the plastic and form it into an 8-inch flat square, then fold the remaining plastic wrap over to cover. Refrigerate for 1 hour.
- On a well-floured surface, roll the dough into a 10-inch square. Place the butter square on top of the dough diagonally (at a 45° angle from the dough square). Fold the dough edges into the middle in an envelope fold.
- Gently roll the envelope out to a large square, then fold the right third into the middle and the left third over that. Turn the dough 90°, roll out it into a flat square, and repeat. Do one more turn, then refrigerate for at least two hours.
- Repeat the turning process four more times, then chill for 1 hour. Your dough is now ready to use.
- For the croissants and assembly:
- Line two baking sheets with parchment paper. Set aside.
- Cut your puff pastry into thirds, lengthwise. Roll out each third to a thickness of 1/4 inch, then cut into 6 equal rectangles, for a total of 18.
- Leaving a 1/2-inch border, place 1/2 ounce milk chocolate on the short side of the edge of the rectangles (not in the middle). Top with mini-marshmallows. If you have a crème brûlée torch, toast the marshmallows gently, as this will keep them from exploding in the oven.
- Gently wrap the pastry dough over the filling and tuck underneath so that the seam is on the bottom. Transfer to a baking sheet. Repeat with the rest of the rectangles until you have 18 croissants, 9 on each baking sheet. (If you plan to freeze these for later, do so now. Flash freeze on the sheet, then wrap each croissant with plastic wrap and place in a freezer bag. Bake directly from the freezer, just add 5 minutes to the baking time.) Cover loosely

with plastic wrap and let rise at room temperature for 1 hour.
- Preheat oven to 400° F. Gently brush each croissant with the beaten egg. Bake for 15 to 20 minutes, turning the baking sheets halfway through, or until they are deeply golden-brown and some of the marshmallow has bubbled out. Let cool for at least 5 minutes. Croissants will keep, in an airtight container at room temperature for about 3 days.

## 89. S'mores Fridge Cake

*Serving: Makes 9 | Prep: | Cook: | Ready in:*

### Ingredients

- 550 grams  Milk chocolate (chips or bars chopped into small pieces)
- 150 grams  Dark chocolate
- 100 grams  Mini marshmallows
- 220 grams  Broken biscuit pieces (I used a mix of malted milk, digestives, bourbons and viennese whirls)

### Direction

- Start by gently melting the chocolates in a large bowl either over a pan of simmering water or in the micro.
- Line your brownie pan with parchment, using a third of melted chocolate pour a layer into the pan, add half of the broken biscuits and a third of the mini marshmallows, cover with a third of the melted chocolate.
- Repeat the process, finish with the remaining marshmallows.
- Place in the fridge for at least 60 minutes, now using a kitchen blowtorch burnish the marshmallows gently, cut into 9 squares, and set in the fridge for a few minutes to firm before serving.

## 90. S'mores Ice Cream

*Serving: Makes 1 quart | Prep: | Cook: | Ready in:*

### Ingredients

- 3 cups  half and half
- 3/4 cup  graham cracker crumbs
- 2 tablespoons  milk powder
- 1 teaspoon  sugar
- 1 pinch  salt
- 5 ounces  bittersweet chocolate, finely chopped
- 1 cup  mini marshmallows

### Direction

- Heat the oven to 250. Spread the graham cracker crumbs on a sheet tray and bake for 10 minutes, or until lightly browned. Let cool for 5-10 minutes.
- In a medium saucepan, warm the milk and cream until just before it hits a simmer. Add the graham cracker crumbs, milk powder, sugar, and salt. Whisk thoroughly to combine, turn off the heat, and let steep for 30 minutes.
- Strain the milk mixture through a fine sieve, pressing on the now-mushy graham crackers to get as much of the liquid out as possible. Discard the solids. Let chill completely and freeze according to your ice cream maker's instructions.
- While the ice cream spins, melt the chocolate over a double boiler, or in 30 second intervals in the microwave. At the last possible minute before the ice cream is done, drizzle in the chocolate in a very thin stream, with the machine still running. This will create thin shards of chocolate throughout the ice cream. If your machine doesn't allow this, stop the motor and stir by hand as you stream in the melted chocolate. If THAT doesn't work, pour a thin layer of ice cream into a freezer container, pour in some chocolate, and repeat until all of the ice cream is packed.
- Fold in the marshmallows, or layer them in as you pack the ice cream into a container. Serve with a graham cracker, marshmallow sauce,

and hot fudge for the ultimate s'mores indulgence.

## 91. S'mores Icebox Cake

*Serving: Makes 1 cake | Prep: | Cook: |Ready in:*

### Ingredients

- For the cake:
- 2 cups heavy cream, divided
- 4 tablespoons mascarpone cheese, divided
- 1 teaspoon vanilla
- 1 sleeve graham crackers (about 9 sheets)
- 1 cup miniature marshmallows
- For the chocolate pudding:
- 2 tablespoons cornstarch
- 1/4 cup sugar
- 1/8 teaspoon salt
- 1/4 cup unsweetened cocoa powder
- 1/2 cup milk
- 1/2 cup cream
- 1/2 teaspoon vanilla

### Direction

- First make the pudding. In a heavy-bottomed medium saucepan, whisk together the cornstarch, sugar, salt, and cocoa powder. Slowly whisk in the milk, cream, and vanilla and bring the mixture to a boil over medium heat. As soon as it boils, reduce to a simmer and cook, whisking constantly, until the mixture begins to thicken (about 3 to 5 minutes). Set aside to cool.
- Whip 1 cup of the heavy cream with 2 tablespoons of the mascarpone and the vanilla until stiff peaks form.
- Line a 9- by 5-inch loaf pan with plastic wrap. Place a layer of graham crackers at the bottom (you will need to break some of them to fit snugly). Follow with a layer of marshmallows, then a layer of mascarpone whipped cream to cover and fill in the spaces between the marshmallows (reserving 1/2 cup for the topping), then a thin layer of cooled chocolate pudding. Repeat the layers until you reach the top of the pan (you should be able to get 3 layers of each), and finish with graham crackers.
- Place plastic wrap over the top of the pan and put the cake in the refrigerator overnight (or for at least 8 hours).
- Remove the cake. Take off the top layer of plastic wrap and invert the cake over a serving platter. Remove the rest of the plastic wrap.
- Whip the remaining cup of cream and 2 tablespoons of mascarpone. Spread this whipped cream over the top and sides of the cake. Top with the remaining marshmallows and briefly toast them using a kitchen torch.

## 92. S'mores Layer Cake

*Serving: Makes one big ol' 8-inch layer cake | Prep: 2hours0mins | Cook: 2hours0mins |Ready in:*

### Ingredients

- 1 GANACHE:
- 4 cups chopped milk chocolate
- 1 1/2 cups heavy cream
- 3 x Graham Cake (https://food52.com/recipes...)
- 2 MARSHMALLOW:
- 2/3 cup cool water, divided (5.35 oz)
- 2 envelopes granulated gelatin (5 teaspoons)
- 2 cups granulated sugar (14.00 oz)
- 1 tablespoon vanilla extract (15 g)

### Direction

- Make the ganache: Place the chocolate in a large, heat-safe bowl. In a medium pot, bring the cream to a simmer over medium heat.
- Pour the hot cream over the chocolate and let sit, undisturbed, for 15 to 20 seconds. Using a silicone spatula, begin stirring in tight circles in the center of the bowl, eventually working in larger circles outward until the ganache is

smooth and glossy. Set aside to cool to a spreadable consistency (20 to 30 minutes) — you can use the fridge or freezer to speed up the process, just keep an eye on it; you don't want it to be liquid anymore or look oozy, but you also don't want it to be hard or difficult to work with. Ideally, it should be spreadable, like thick frosting!

- The marshmallow needs to be used right away once it is made, so before you begin to mix it, get everything ready to assemble the cake. Working one cake layer at a time, scoop 1 cup of ganache into the center of the cake, and spread into an even layer — the ganache will fill the slightly sunken cavity of the cake, but continue to spread it nearly to the edges. Repeat on all cake layers, and set aside. Transfer the remaining ganache to a disposable pastry bag and cut a 1/4-inch opening from the tip. Set aside.
- Grease a silicone spatula with nonstick spray. Grease the inside of a disposable pastry bag with nonstick spray. You can fit it with a large round tip, or just cut a 1/2-inch opening from the end. I find it can be handy to have a pair of kitchen scissors handy — spray them with nonstick spray too!
- Pour 1/3 cup cool water into a medium, shallow dish and sprinkle the gelatin even over the surface. Let bloom for 5 minutes.
- Pour the remaining 1/3 cup water and the sugar into a medium pot. Heat the pot over medium-high heat. Stir the mixture until it comes to a boil, then stop stirring completely: Agitating a boiling sugar syrup can encourage crystals to form, which can lead to disaster. Once you stop stirring, brush any visible sugar crystals away from the sides of the pot with a damp pastry brush.
- Once the mixture begins to boil, fasten a candy thermometer to the side of the pot. Continue to boil until the temperature reads 245° F.
- Pour the syrup into the bowl of an electric mixer fitted with the whisk attachment. Add the vanilla and let the mixture cool to 220° F.
- While the syrup cools, melt the bloomed gelatin, either in the microwave (15 to 20 seconds) or over a double boiler, until it is fluid.
- When the sugar syrup has cooled, add it to the bowl of your mixer and gradually work the mixer up to medium speed. Once the mixer is running, add the melted gelatin (and any extracts, if using). Whip the sugar on medium speed until the bowl feels almost entirely cool to the touch and the sugar is opaque white and very fluffy, 4 to 5 minutes. It should hold stiff peaks. Try not to stop and restart the mixer multiple times, just keep whipping steadily for 4 to 5 minutes.
- While the marshmallow whips, place one layer of the cake on a cake turntable (or straight onto a cake stand). Have the other two layers ready to go.
- When the marshmallow is fully aerated (it should hold peaks), use the greased spatula to transfer it to the greased pastry bag. Starting in the center of the first cake layer, pipe a spiral of marshmallow, working to the outside edge. Stop about 1/4 inch from the edge. If desired, toast the marshmallow layer with a kitchen torch, then top with the next cake layer. Repeat this process with another cake layer, then place the final cake layer on top.
- For the top of the cake, pipe little rounds/drops of marshmallow all over the top of the cake. If you want, use the scissors to help snip the end of each piped piece to help release it from the bag. Once the surface is totally covered, toast it all over with a torch.
- Drizzle the remaining ganache over the surface of the cake. Let the cake stand 15 minutes to 20 minutes before slicing and serving.

## 93. S'mores Pie

*Serving: Serves 8 | Prep: | Cook: | Ready in:*

### Ingredients

- 14 ounces milk chocolate

- 3/4 cup heavy cream
- 1 9" prepared graham cracker crust
- 10-15 marshmallows

## Direction

- Combine chocolate and heavy cream in a microwave-safe bowl and heat on high for 2½ minutes. Stir until the chocolate is melted and you have a gorgeous ganache!
- Pour into a 9" prepared graham cracker crust.
- Cover with plastic wrap and park in the fridge for at least 4 hours or overnight.
- Cut marshmallows in half on the bias. Place the marshmallows cut side down on the chilled pie.
- Pre-heat broiler and pop in the oven for about 1 minute, rotating pan and watching closely so the marshmallows don't burn. Let cool and cover with plastic wrap. Chill for another hour or two to let ganache set again.
- Slice and serve. This pie is so rich and delicious, a small slice will satisfy your sweet tooth.

## 94. S'mores Pop Tart Slab Pie

*Serving: Serves 25 | Prep: | Cook: | Ready in:*

### Ingredients

- For the pie crust:
- 7 1/2 cups all-purpose flour
- 6 tablespoons granulated sugar
- 1 teaspoon kosher salt
- 1 1/3 cups cold unsalted butter (NOT room temperature), cut into pieces
- 1 1/3 cups cold shortening (NOT room temperature)
- 1 1/3 cups ice water
- 4 teaspoons distilled white vinegar
- For the marshmallow fluff and chocolate filling:
- 3/4 cup granulated sugar
- 1/2 cup light corn syrup
- 1/4 cup water
- 1/8 teaspoon kosher salt
- 2 large egg whites, at room temperature
- 1/4 teaspoon cream of tartar
- 1 1/2 teaspoons vanilla extract
- 1/2 cup unsweetened cocoa powder
- 2/3 cup heavy cream
- 1 1/3 cups dark chocolate, chopped (or dark chocolate chips)
- 1/4 cup granulated sugar
- 2 tablespoons butter, cubed
- 1 pinch kosher salt
- 4 graham crackers, crushed
- 1 egg plus 1 tablespoon water, lightly beaten
- 7 to 8 ounces mini marshmallows, with some reserved for decorating

## Direction

- For the pie crust:
- Whisk together the flour, sugar, and salt in a large bowl or the bowl of your food processor. (I used my food processor, but I didn't always have one and have had great results making this crust by hand.) Please note that this is basically a double pie, meaning it is a lot of dough! I did mine in two batches—that is, I divided the recipe in half and repeated the process twice. If you have a giant mixing bowl or food processor, go for it, but my equipment isn't large enough to handle 7 1/2 cups of flour.
- Add in the chopped pieces of cold butter and cold shortening. Blend together with your hands or pulse with your processor until you have coarse crumbs (it doesn't have to be perfect). You can use a pastry cutter, too, but I find that a clean pair of hands work best. Mix together the water and vinegar in a small bowl. When ready, slowly drizzle it over the dough, a tablespoon or so at a time, gently stirring the mixture with a fork or pulsing with your processor, until fully incorporated (you may not use all of the liquid).
- It might seem a bit too wet at this point, but it will dry up while it sits in the fridge. Form the dough gently into 2 loose balls, wrap tightly in

plastic wrap, and chill in the fridge for a minimum of 3 hours or overnight (as always, overnight is best). Make your filling when you are almost ready to use your dough.
- For the marshmallow fluff and chocolate filling:
- For the marshmallow fluff: Stir together the sugar, corn syrup, water, and salt in a small saucepan over high heat. Bring the mixture to a boil, stirring often, until it reaches 240° F on a candy/fat thermometer. Be careful not to let the mixture bubble over — turn the heat down if you need to and keep a watchful eye over it. This might take a little longer than you think, but just keep at it. Mine took about 10 minutes, but when you're standing there watching it, it feels like an eternity. It got stuck at around 220° for what seemed like forever, but then it eventually got up to 240°.
- Meanwhile, place the egg whites and cream of tartar in the bowl of a stand mixer fitted with a whisk attachment. Start whipping the egg whites to soft peaks on medium speed. You want to have the egg whites whipped and ready to go, waiting for your syrup to be drizzled in. If they're whipping faster than your syrup is coming to temperature, just stop the mixer until the syrup is ready, which is what I did.
- When the syrup reaches 240° F, reduce the mixer speed to low and slowly drizzle about 2 tablespoons of syrup into the egg whites to warm them. If you add too much syrup at once, the whites will scramble. Slowly drizzle in the rest of the syrup, a bit at a time — seriously, do not do more than 2 tablespoons at a time.
- Increase the speed to medium high and whip until the marshmallow fluff is stiff and glossy, about 7 solid minutes. Don't try to speed this process up! Add in the vanilla and whip 2 minutes more. Use the fluff immediately or refrigerate stored in an airtight container for up to 2 weeks. (I made my fluff about 4 hours ahead of time before baking with it, and I actually doubled the recipe so that I'd have some extra to spread of the top of the pie pieces... just an idea!)
- For the chocolate filling: If you have a double boiler, use that. I don't, so I just melt chocolate very slowly and carefully because it burns easily. In a saucepan, combine your cocoa powder, heavy cream, chocolate, sugar, butter, and salt. Stir constantly medium-low heat constantly until everything is melted and smooth. Remove from the heat and set aside. The mixture will thicken up as it cools down, making it easy to spread over your pie crust later.
- For assembly: Remove your crust from the refrigerator to allow for easier rolling. Preheat your oven to 400° F. Generously butter a half-sheet pan. Roll out your first ball of dough — it should be about an inch or two longer and wider than the baking sheet, but it does not have to be perfect by any means. If you need to re-roll a few scraps here and there to patch up pieces, that's fine. Move it over onto the baking sheet by draping it over the rolling pin. Unfold it and gently press the pie crust into the bottom of the baking sheet.
- Spread your chocolate mixture over the dough, then scatter mini marshmallows over top, saving some for a finishing touch once the pie is baked. Sprinkle 4 crushed graham crackers over the top of the marshmallow. Roll out your second pie crust and gently place it over the top. Crimp the edges together, discarding any scraps (or using them to decorate the pie, dealer's choice). Pull the dough slightly inward, away from the edges of the baking sheet, to make it easier to cut later.
- Use a fork to make a pattern in the top of the pie, like a traditional Pop-Tart. Beat together your egg and water and brush the top of the pie with it. Place the pie in the oven, then reduce the heat to 375° F. Bake for 50 to 60 minutes, until golden brown and shiny on top. Remove from the oven and allow to cool completely.
- Spread the marshmallow fluff all over the top of the pie and decorate with any leftover mini

marshmallows. Use a kitchen torch to brûlée your topping, then slice, serve, and enjoy!

## 95. S'mores Cake

*Serving: Serves 12 | Prep: | Cook: |Ready in:*

### Ingredients

- Cake
- 1 1/2 cups  cups graham cracker crumbs (about 15 whole crackers ground in processor)
- 1/2 cup  all-purpose flour
- 2 1/2 teaspoons  baking powder
- 1/2 cup  unsalted butter, room temp
- 3/4 cup  sugar
- 2  large eggs
- 1 teaspoon  vanilla extract
- 3/4 cup  whole milk
- Frosting and Ganache
- 16 ounces  bittersweet chocolate (do not exceed 61% cacao), chopped
- 1 cup  (scant) heavy whipping cream
- 1 cup  unsalted butter, room temp
- 1 cup  confectioners sugar
- 1/4 teaspoon  vanilla extract
- 1 cup  marshmallow fluff
- 3/4 cup  marshmallows

### Direction

- Preheat oven to 350°F. Lightly butter 3 9" round cake pans. Cut 3 parchment rounds to fit snugly into the bottom of each pan and place them on top of the buttered pan.
- Whisk graham crumbs, flour, baking powder, and pinch of salt in medium bowl. Beat 1/2 c. butter and sugar in large bowl until light and fluffy. Add eggs 1 at a time, beating to blend between additions. Beat in vanilla.
- Add graham-cracker mixture in 3 additions alternately with milk in 2 additions, beginning and ending with graham-cracker mixture. Divide batter among pans and bake for 20-25 minutes, until a toothpick inserted in comes out clean. Transfer to a cooling rack, wait ten minutes and then invert the cakes out of the pans to cool completely.
- To make the frosting, beat the butter until fluffy. Then, beat in one-fourth of the sugar until fluffy, then repeat with the remaining sugar. Beat in the vanilla, then stir in the marshmallow cream until well blended.
- To make the ganache, place chocolate in medium bowl. Bring cream just to boil in small saucepan; pour over chocolate. Let stand 1 minute; stir until smooth. Cool ganache until lukewarm.
- Assemble the cake: Place one layer of graham cracker cake on your stand. Spread a layer of ganache on top, going 1/8" away from the edges of the cake, then place into the fridge for 5 minutes to allow the ganache to harden. Top with a layer of marshmallow frosting. Repeat with the second layer, then top with the final cake layer. Spread the remaining ganache over the cake. Work quickly so it doesn't cool down while you're still spreading it, which can make for an ugly cake. While the ganache is still soft, press the marshmallows onto the top of the cake. Put cake in the fridge for at least 30 minutes to let the ganache harden up. Finally, the fun part! Take that baby out of the fridge, turn on your kitchen torch and brown the marshmallows on top, being careful not to melt the ganache, until perfectly campfire brown. If you notice the ganache is looking pretty shiny and soft, put the cake into the fridge for 5 minutes before continuing to torch the cake. Store cake in the fridge but let come to room temperature for at least an hour before serving. YUM!

## 96. Sally's S'Mores

*Serving: Makes about 32 | Prep: | Cook: |Ready in:*

### Ingredients

- The cookies: Wheat Germ Butterscotch Slices

- 3 c sifted flour
- 1 T baking powder
- ½ tsp salt
- 3 T wheat germ
- 1 c butter, softened
- 1 ¼ c firmly packed dark brown sugar
- 1 tsp vanilla
- 2 eggs
- The S'Mores
- 1 batch Wheat Germ Butterscotch Slices
- 1 batch Marshmallows
- Chocolate Ganache, see below
- Peach, Strawberry, Raspberry or other jam of your choice

## Direction

- The cookies: Wheat Germ Butterscotch Slices
- Sift together flour, baking powder, salt and wheat germ
- Cream butter and gradually beat in brown sugar, vanilla, and then add eggs, one at a time
- Stir in flour mixture
- Shape into 2 rolls about 2" in diameter and wrap each in waxed paper or plastic wrap. Chill thoroughly in refrigerator
- Preheat oven to 400
- Cut chilled roll into 1/8" slices, and bake on greased cookie sheet (or on cookie sheet lined with parchment)
- Bake for 7 or 8 minutes, so that they're cooked through, but still soft and on the underdone side. Run a spatula under them right away, let cool on the pan for a minute or two, and then finish cooling on racks
- The S'Mores
- The Marshmallows: Make one batch notlazy. Rustic's marshmallows, but omit the chocolate, cocoa, and cinnamon. Cut into 2" x 2" x 1" pieces.
- The Chocolate Ganache: ½ lb. dark chocolate, 1/3 c heavy whipping cream: Heat whipping cream, to warm but not boiling. Melt chocolate. I use the microwave for this, heating on a med-low setting until the chocolate just begins to melt, and then stirring until completely melted. Add whipping cream to chocolate a few tablespoons at a time, stirring and stirring until it is all incorporated. Cool to room temperature. As it cools, it will thicken to a nice, spreadable consistency.
- To make the S'mores: Spread one cookie with Chocolate Ganache another with jam. Either toast the marshmallow, skewered, on the flame of your stove or grill, or microwave it for a few seconds until puffed and soft. Sandwich toasted marshmallow between chocolate cookie and jam cookie, and eat it right away.

## 97. Salted Toffee & Brown Butter Crispy Treats

*Serving: Makes 16 2-inch treats  | Prep:  | Cook: |Ready in:*

## Ingredients

- 4 ounces (1 stick) unsalted butter, plus extra for the pan
- 1 10-ounce bag marshmallows
- 1/2 tsp sea salt (level, not heaping)
- 6 cups puffed rice cereal (about half a 12-ounce box)
- 2/3 cup English toffee bits (can substitute very finely chopped English toffee bars)

## Direction

- Butter (or coat with non-stick spray) an 8-inch square pan.
- In a large bowl, combine the cereal, sea salt and toffee bits. Toss to mix well.
- In a large pot over medium heat (one big enough to hold six cups of cereal), cook the butter until it turns brown and smells nutty, about 4 to 6 minutes. Be sure to stir frequently, scraping up any bits from the bottom.
- When the butter is browned, turn the heat as low as it will go and stir in the marshmallows. Stir until they've thoroughly melted and are

smooth; you shouldn't see any marshmallow shapes at this point.

- Remove the pot from the stove. Add the cereal-salt-toffee to the marshmallows, mixing quickly until evenly incorporated. (A strong, silicon spatula works well.) Spread into prepared pan, pressing firmly and evenly. A piece of waxed paper sprayed with oil works well for pressing and spreading the cereal into the corners and edges.
- Let cool and cut into squares. Share them right away, lest risk eating the whole pan by yourself.

## 98. Sheet Pan S'mores

*Serving: Serves 8-10 | Prep: 0hours20mins | Cook: 0hours5mins | Ready in:*

### Ingredients

- 1/2 cup heavy cream
- 1/2 tablespoon unsalted butter
- 1/2 cup semisweet chocolate chips
- 2  4 1/2-ounce sleeves graham crackers, broken into halves
- 1  10-ounce bag mini marshmallows

### Direction

- Preheat the broiler to low. Position the oven rack so it's 6 inches away from the heating element.
- Bring a small saucepan of water to a boil and then reduce the heat to maintain a simmer. Place the cream, butter, and chocolate chips in a large heatproof bowl and set it over the saucepan (make sure the bottom of the bowl doesn't touch the water). Stir the mixture until the butter and chocolate have melted, about 5 minutes. Turn off the heat but leave the bowl over the saucepan to keep the sauce warm.
- Place half the graham cracker halves on a baking sheet and top with half the marshmallows. Broil just until the marshmallows turn golden brown, about 1 minute, depending on the strength of your broiler. Place the remaining graham crackers and marshmallows on top and broil one more time until the second layer of marshmallows is golden brown (or burnt, if you prefer that!), about 1 minute more.
- Drizzle the warm chocolate sauce over the "nachos" and serve straight from the pan, with plenty of napkins handy.

## 99. Spooky Halloween Popcorn Balls

*Serving: Makes 12 | Prep: | Cook: | Ready in:*

### Ingredients

- 12 cups Popped popcorn
- 2 tablespoons Butter or margine
- 6 cups Mini marshmallows
- 1 teaspoon Orange food coloring
- Butter or margarine(for hands)
- 12 Candy eyeballs in wrappers
- 24 Candy gummi worms

### Direction

- Put popcorn into a large bowl.
- In a medium size sauce pan, melt butter over low heat.
- Add marshmallows.
- With a wooden spoon, stir marshmallows until melted.
- Turn off heat.
- Stir in food coloring.
- Stir well.
- Pour marshmallow mixture over popcorn.
- Stir until popcorn is well coated.
- Butter hands well for each popcorn ball.
- Shape into 12 medium popcorn balls.
- Put on serving plate.
- Put one candy eyeball on top of each popcorn ball.
- Push in just a little.

- Arrange two candy gummi worms on top of each popcorn balls.

## 100. Spumoni Rocky Road

*Serving: Makes about 36 squares, depending on your cut | Prep: | Cook: |Ready in:*

### Ingredients

- MARSHMALLOWS
- Note: only about half of this recipe will be needed for the rocky road
- Candy thermometer, Cooking spray
- 3 packages of dry gelatin (will use 2-1/2 tablespoons of it)
- 1/2 cup warm water
- 1-2/3 cups superfine sugar
- 1/2 cup plus 1-1/2 teaspoons white corn syrup
- 1/3 cup water, extra
- 1-1/2 tablespoon rose petal jelly (or 1 teaspoon rosewater). Note: I originally used rosewater but rose petal jelly is my preference.
- 3/4 cup powdered sugar, sifted – to be used for garnish
- ROCKY ROAD - This Rocky Road is made without tempering the chocolate:
- 18ozs total chocolate = 10ozs 70% dark chocolate and 8oz semi sweet chocolate
- 3-4 cups homemade rose flavored marshmallows cut into bite size pieces
- 1-1/2 cup pistachio halves and pieces   - unsalted or lightly salted
- 1/4 cup finely minced tart cherries
- A baking sheet lined with parchment paper that has been lightly sprayed with cooking spray

### Direction

- MARSHMALLOWS
- Lightly spray cooking spray onto an 8x8 inch cake pans and line with parchment paper. Sift about 3 tablespoons powdered sugar onto the parchment, set aside.
- Place 2-1/2 tablespoons of the gelatin and warm water in the bowl of an electric mixer fitted with a whisk attachment. Stir well to combine and set aside.
- Place the sugar, syrup and extra water in a 2 quart saucepan over medium heat. Bring to a boil and cook without stirring until a candy thermometer has reached the soft ball stage (115°C/240°F) – about 10 minutes. Remove from the heat.
- With the mixer running at high speed, gradually add the hot syrup to the gelatin mixture. Beat for 10 minutes or until the mixture is thick and fluffy. Add the rose flavoring and beat to combine about 30 seconds more.
- Scrape the marshmallow into your previously prepared pan, spread as smooth as possible with a damp rubber spatula. Dust the top with sifted powdered sugar, let stand uncovered at room temperature until set…up to 12 hours.
- Invert the marshmallow onto a cutting board that has been dusted with powdered sugar. Peel off the parchment; it will be sticky, dust with sifted powdered sugar. Cut into bite size squares (for rocky road) with a sharp knife or kitchen shears. Dip the sides in powdered sugar, shake off excess and store in an airtight container up to two weeks.
- ROCKY ROAD - This Rocky Road is made without tempering the chocolate:
- Slowly melt 10ozs of the chocolate in a microwave at 50% power, stir to help the melting process after each minute.
- When the chocolate has just about melted, stir in the last 8ozs, microwave for 30 seconds at 50% power.
- Remove from the microwave and stir until the chocolate mixture is completely melted and smooth.
- Quickly stir in the nuts and cherries and then gently but quickly fold in the marshmallows to coat.
- Spread the mixture onto the prepared baking sheet, square off and if needed, press down to

smooth the top. Let dry at room temperature, 4 hours to overnight.
- With a sharp knife, cut into pieces and store in an airtight container up to a week.

## 101. Strawberry Cheesecake Rice Krispie Treats

*Serving: Makes 16 | Prep: | Cook: | Ready in:*

### Ingredients

- 10.5 ounces bag strawberry flavored marshmallows
- 3 tablespoons butter
- 6 cups rice krispies cereal
- 1 cup chopped graham crackers
- 1 cup white chocolate chips
- 1 tablespoon cheesecake pudding mix

### Direction

- Melt marshmallows and butter either a) in a medium pot on the stove or b) in a large microwave-safe bowl. Remove from heat or the microwave and stir in rice krispies and graham crackers.
- Press mixture evenly into a 9 by 12 inch pan lined with aluminum foil. Let cool until firm and then cut into squares.
- Add white chocolate to a medium microwave safe bowl and heat in 20 second intervals until melted and smooth. Stir in cheesecake pudding mix until well incorporated, and then drizzle over rice krispie treats. Top with sprinkles, if desired.

## 102. Strawberry S'mores Sundae

*Serving: Makes 4 sundaes | Prep: | Cook: | Ready in:*

### Ingredients

- 6 ounces semisweet chocolate
- 1/2 cup heavy cream
- 8 marshmallows
- 1 pint the best strawberry ice cream you can get your hands on
- 2/3 cup graham cracker crumbs (take out some rage on a sealed plastic bag of crackers until they reach the size you want on your ice cream; I like them somewhere between the Nerds candy and dust)

### Direction

- Whisk the chocolate into the cream over low heat until smooth. Cook and whisk for 2 to 3 minutes; sauce will thicken slightly. Remove from heat and set aside.
- Roast marshmallows by sticking them on the end of a long skewer and cooking them over your stovetop burner (or an open flame, if you have one handy). If you'd just like to crisp those bad boys up to your liking and then plop them on top of your ice cream, you are more than welcome to do so. If you'd like to get a little more involved (spoiler: I did, because I left 'mallow duty to a boy who SAID he had a PLAN), try this:
- Cut two marshmallows into about three pieces each, and stick the pieces evenly amongst the tines of a fork. Place 'mallows into your flame until it starts to get roasty and melt. Then, using a big spoon or another fork, fold that mess in on itself a few times, continuously roasting the outside. This gets the crispy, roasty flavor all throughout the marshmallow layer, interspersed with melt gooeyness. Scrape the goods from your (extremely sticky) utensils directly onto your sundae.
- Scoop ice cream into individual bowls. Top with a not-shy drizzle of chocolate sauce, a generous sprinkling of graham cracker crumbs, and the smashed and roasted marshmallows.

## 103. Stuffed With Fluff Mars Bar Cupcakes

*Serving: Makes 24 cupcakes | Prep: | Cook: |Ready in:*

### Ingredients

- Chocolate Cupcake Ingredients
- 3/4 cup boiling water
- 2/4 cup cocoa powder, sifted
- 3/4 cup butter, softened
- 2 cups sugar
- 3 large eggs
- 1 teaspoon vanilla extract
- 2 1/2 cups cake flour
- 1 teaspoon baking soda
- 1 teaspoon baking powder
- 1/2 teaspoon kosher salt
- 1 cup buttermilk
- 1 cup chopped Mars Bars
- Chocolate Icing and Filing
- 1 cup butter, softened
- 1/2 cup cocoa powder, sifted
- 2 1/2 cups icing sugar
- 3 tablespoons milk
- 24 tablespoons marshmallow fluff (Filing)

### Direction

- 1) For the cupcakes, preheat oven to 350°F. Line 24 muffin cups with paper liners and spray with non-stick cooking spray.
- 2) In a small bowl, combine boiling water and cocoa powder. Set aside. In a medium bowl, sift together cake flour, baking soda, baking powder and salt.
- 3) Using an electric mixer, cream butter and sugar until light and fluffy. Add eggs one at a time, beating well after each addition. Continue creaming on medium speed and add vanilla extract. On low speed, alternate adding flour mixture and buttermilk, beginning and ending with the flour. Add cocoa mixture and chopped Mars bars, continuing on low speed, just until all ingredients are combined. Spoon batter into prepared cupcake liners until each is ¾ full. Bake 22-24 minutes or until tops feel firm and a toothpick inserted in the center comes out clean.
- Ingredients: Chocolate Cupcake: ¾ cup boiling water, ¾ cup cocoa powder, sifted ¾ cup butter, softened 2 cups sugar, 3 large eggs, 1 tsp vanilla extract, 2 ½ cups cake flour, 1 tsp baking soda, 1 tsp baking powder, ½ tsp kosher salt, 1 cup buttermilk, 1 cup chopped Mars Bars
- Chocolate Icing: 1 cup butter, softened; ½ cup cocoa powder, sifted; 2 ½ cups icing sugar; 3 tbsp. milk
- Filing: 24 tbsp. marshmallow fluff
- 1) For the cupcakes, preheat oven to 350°F. Line 24 muffin cups with paper liners and spray with non-stick cooking spray.
- 2) In a small bowl, combine boiling water and cocoa powder. Set aside. In a medium bowl, sift together cake flour, baking soda, baking powder and salt.
- 3) Using an electric mixer, cream butter and sugar until light and fluffy. Add eggs one at a time, beating well after each addition. Continue creaming on medium speed and add vanilla extract. On low speed, alternate adding flour mixture and buttermilk, beginning and ending with the flour. Add cocoa mixture and chopped Mars bars, continuing on low speed, just until all ingredients are combined. Spoon batter into prepared cupcake liners until each is ¾ full. Bake 22-24 minutes or until tops feel firm and a toothpick inserted in the center comes out clean.
- 4) For the icing, in an electric mixer, combine butter, cocoa powder and icing sugar on low speed. Once combined, on medium speed, add milk 1 tbsp. at a time to achieve desired consistency.
- 5) To assemble the cupcakes, using a paring knife, cut out a small cone from the center of each cupcake. Coat a spoon with non-stick cooking spray and spoon 1 heaping tbsp. of marshmallow fluff into each cupcake. Replace cut-out piece of cupcake. Spread cupcake top with chocolate icing and serve.

## 104. Swedish Princess Cake

*Serving: Makes one domed 9-inch cake | Prep: 1hours0mins | Cook: 0hours40mins |Ready in:*

### Ingredients

- Vanilla Custard
- 2 cups whole milk (500g)
- 2 vanilla beans, split with seeds scraped out
- 6 egg yolks
- 1/2 cup 2 tablespoon sugar (120g)
- 1/4 cup 1 tablespoon cornstarch (40g)
- 4 tablespoons unsalted butter, cubed (50g)
- Sponge Cake, Fillings, & Decorations
- 4 eggs
- 3/4 cup sugar (150g) + 2 tablespoons
- 1/3 cup cornstarch, sifted (50g)
- 3/4 cup all purpose flour (110g)
- 1 teaspoon baking powder (6g)
- 1/2 teaspoon salt (3g)
- 1 teaspoon almond extract
- 4 tablespoons unsalted butter, melted and cooled (50g)
- 2 1/2 cups heavy whipping cream (600ml)
- 3 tablespoons jam (I used raspberry, but use whatever you like)
- 1 pound marzipan, store-bought or homemade
- 1/2 cup mini marshmallows
- 1/2 cup powdered sugar
- 1 Red food coloring (gel, not liquid)
- 1 Green food coloring (gel, not liquid)
- 1 Powdered sugar (for dusting)
- 3 ounces bittersweet chocolate
- 3 tablespoons sugar (50g)

### Direction

- For the Custard: In a pot over medium heat, heat the milk with the vanilla beans and seeds just until it starts to simmer. Turn off the heat and let it sit. Mix egg yolks, cornstarch, sugar, and a pinch of salt in a bowl. Remove vanilla pods from milk and slowly pour milk into bowl, stirring constantly. Return to the pot and whisk 4 to 5 minutes, until very thick. Add butter and stir until melted. Refrigerate for at least one hour, or up to overnight.
- For the Cake: Preheat the oven to 350 °F, 175 °C. Butter or spray a 9-inch springform pan. Line the bottom of the pan with a parchment circle, then butter or spray that as well. In the bowl of a KitchenAid or electric mixer fitted with a whisk attachment, beat eggs and 3/4 cup sugar until very thick, pale, and fluffy, about 5 to 7 minutes. Add almond extract. Sift flour, cornstarch, salt, and baking powder over bowl (or sift into a separate bowl first) and fold in with a spatula. Fold in the melted butter and stir just to combine. Pour batter into prepared pan and bake for 20 to 30 minutes, or until a toothpick comes out clean. Let the cake cool in the pan for 5 minutes before turning it out onto a rack to cool completely.
- Make the Fondant Rose: Make the fondant by microwaving the marshmallows until melted (15-20 seconds). Stir in the powdered sugar and knead for a few minutes on a clean surface, adding more powdered sugar if it sticks, adding a few drops of water if it's too dry, until smooth and pliable. Knead in red food coloring drop by drop until you have your desired shade of pink. Dust two small pieces of parchment or waxed paper with powdered sugar and one by one, place the balls of fondant between the sheets of greaseproof paper and flatten each ball out with your fingers, to a thin circle, approximately 2 cm/1 in in diameter, to form the petals. Roll the first petal up to form a center bud and wrap the remaining petals around the bud to make a rose. Leave to dry at room temperature for at least an hour.
- When the cake is completely cool, use a serrated knife to carefully slice it into three even layers. Divide the jam evenly between the first two layers, spreading a thin layer over the top. Next, add the remaining 2 tablespoons of sugar to the whipped cream and beat until it holds stiff peaks. Fold half of the whipped cream into the pastry cream, reserving the

other half. Evenly divide the pastry-whipped cream mixture between the first two layers, spreading it carefully over the thin jam layer.
- Stack the two first layers, then top with the remaining cake slice. Set aside one cup of the reserved whipped cream, then use a rubber spatula to shape the remaining whipped cream into a dome shape on top of the cake, then set the whole thing into the fridge for an hour to set.
- While the cake is chilling, make the green marzipan exterior. On a surface lightly dusted with powdered sugar, knead the marzipan until it's pliable. Add two dots of green gel food coloring and knead until the color is uniform. If you like, add another dot or two of food coloring until it reaches a light lime color. Place the marzipan between two sheets of waxed paper and roll into a 16-inch diameter circle, large enough to generously cover the cake.
- Take the cake out of the fridge and gently drape the marzipan over the whipped cream dome. Shape and smooth the marzipan around the cake to get a clean appearance. Trim the edges and tuck them neatly under the cake. Fill a pastry bag fitted with a small star tip with the reserved cup of whipped cream, and pipe a row of stars around the edge of the cake to hide any imperfections.
- Melt the bittersweet chocolate in a double boiler or in the microwave (in 10-second increments). Make a skinny-tipped cone with parchment paper and fill it with the melted chocolate, then snip off the tip to create a makeshift pastry bag. Carefully pipe the chocolate over the top of the cake in a swirl or curlicue. Top with the pink rose in the center.

## 105. Sweet Cherries & Creme Puffs

*Serving: Serves 3 dozen | Prep: | Cook: | Ready in:*

### Ingredients

- 1 can non-stick cooking spray
- 1/2 cup unsalted butter
- 1/4 teaspoon kosher salt
- 1 cup water
- 1 cup all-purpose flour
- 4 large eggs
- 8 ounces cream cheese, softened
- 1 cup powdered sugar
- 1/4 cup marshmallow creme
- 1/8 teaspoon almond extract
- 1 cup whipped cream
- 1 cup (about 7 oz. unpitted) pitted and finely chopped fresh sweet cherries, drained

### Direction

- Heat oven to 400 degrees. Spray a large cookie sheet with cooking spray. Set aside.
- Bring butter, salt, and water to a boil in 1-quart saucepan over medium-high heat. Stir in flour.
- Remove from heat and beat on low speed until mixture pulls away from edge of pan. Cool for 5 minutes.
- Beat in eggs one at a time. Beat until smooth.
- Drop teaspoonfuls 2-inches apart onto prepared cookie sheet. Bake for 20 minutes. Reduce heat to 350 degrees and bake for 10-12 minutes more until dry. Remove from oven and cool completely.
- Meanwhile, for filling, beat cream cheese and powdered sugar in a small mixing bowl on low speed until smooth. Beat in marshmallow crème and extract. Fold in whipped cream. Chill for 1 hour or until serving time.
- Just before serving, stir cherries into filling mixture. Cut a slit in the side of each cooled puff and fill with filling mixture. Serve immediately. Makes 3 dozen.

## 106. Sweet Potato Sinfulness

*Serving: Serves 10 | Prep: | Cook: | Ready in:*

## Ingredients

- 8 sweet potatoes
- 3 cups granulated sugar
- 2 teaspoons vanilla
- 2 large eggs
- 1.5 tablespoons cinnamon
- 2 sticks unsalted butter, melted
- 1 bag miniature marshmallows

## Direction

- Microwave the sweet potatoes on High for 15 minutes, then flip them over and microwave for another 12 minutes.
- Remove the potatoes (careful, they're hot and might be making a cute screaming noise). Place them, one by one, on a plate and split them in half lengthwise. Scoop out the insides and place in the bowl of an electric mixer. Don't scrape completely down to the skin. Repeat with all potatoes. Scrap the skins.
- Pour the sugar, vanilla, eggs, cinnamon and melted butter over the potatoes. The sugar should be covering up all the potatoes; you should see no orange (really!). If you do see orange, pour in more sugar until it disappears :)
- Mix all of the ingredients together at medium speed until well combined. The consistency should be more runny than stiff.
- Pour into a 9 x 13 baking dish and bake in a 375 degree oven for 30 minutes.
- Remove the casserole from the oven and pour the entire bag of marshmallows on top, spreading them around with your fingers so every centimeter is covered.
- Set the oven to High Broil and place the casserole under the broiler for no more than a minute. KEEP A CLOSE EYE DURING THIS STEP. The mallows should be lightly browned on top and gaining a glossy sheen. Remove as soon as they begin to head for a burn.
- Allow the casserole to cool for at least 10 minutes before serving.

## 107. Sweet Potato Soufflé

*Serving: Serves 12 | Prep: | Cook: |Ready in:*

## Ingredients

- 6 large sweet potatoes
- 1 teaspoon olive oil
- 1 large navel orange
- 1/2 stick of butter, softened on the counter
- 2 eggs
- 2 tablespoons light brown sugar
- 1 teaspoon ground cinnamon
- 1 teaspoon ground nutmeg
- 1 teaspoon ground ginger
- 1 pinch salt
- 28 large (not jumbo) "jet-puffed" marshmallows
- 1 large sheet pan
- 1 2 quart casserole dish
- 1 blender, big enough to hold 9 cups

## Direction

- Set the oven to 400.
- Rinse and dry the sweet potatoes. Prick each sweet potato with a fork a few times. Rub each sweet potato with just enough olive oil to lightly coat the skin.
- Set the sweet potatoes on the large sheet pan and roast untouched for 30 minutes.
- After 30 minutes, flip the sweet potatoes and continue roasting for an additional 40 minutes, until the jackets are easily pierced with a knife. Remove the sweet potatoes from the oven, slice each one down the middle long ways, and allow them to cool on the counter until easily handled.
- Set the oven to 350.
- Zest the orange until you have about two heaping tablespoons of orange zest.
- Cut the orange into quarters and juice each wedge. A large orange should yield a little over a 1/2 cup of fresh orange juice.
- Measure the sugar, salt, and spices into a small cup.

- Cut just a tiny bit of softened butter from the end of the softened stick and use that to grease the inside of the casserole dish. Reserve the rest for the soufflé.
- Carefully remove the skins and any rough or stringy bits from each sweet potato, dropping each peeled potato into the blender.
- In the blender, add the orange juice and butter to the sweet potatoes. Pulse until smooth.
- Add sugar, salt, and spices into the blended sweet potatoes. Pulse until distributed.
- Crack two eggs into a small cup and make sure to remove any small shelly bits. Drop the eggs into the blender on top of the sweet potato mixture and pulse until just distributed.
- Working quickly, pour the sweet potato mixture into the casserole dish, scraping down the sides of the blender and smoothing the top of the prepared mixture with a spatula.
- Bake the soufflé for 30 minutes or until the peaks have started to brown just slightly.
- Remove the casserole and keep warm until ready to serve.
- About 5 minutes before you're ready to serve, stick the marshmallows evenly across the top of the soufflé. (My 2 quart Pyrex fits exactly 28 marshmallows in seven rows of four).
- Turn the broiler on 'HI.' Have some oven mitts handy. Place the casserole under the broiler, watching carefully, for just 1-2 minutes for the marshmallows to toast but not burn.

## 108. Sympathy For The Devil's Food Cake

*Serving: Serves 2 sinners or 8 saints | Prep: | Cook: | Ready in:*

### Ingredients

- Sweet Spice
- 1 tablespoon ground ginger
- 1 tablespoon ground cinnamon
- 2 teaspoons ground cloves
- 1/2 teaspoon Grains of Paradise, or white peppercorns, or black peppercorns, crushed
- Cake
- 1 1/2 cups all-purpose unbleached flour
- 1 cup granulated sugar
- 7 tablespoons natural cocoa powder, not Dutched
- 1/2 teaspoon baking soda
- 1/2 teaspoon kosher salt
- 2 teaspoons sweet spice mix
- 1/2 cup Guinness Stout
- 1/2 cup espresso or strong black coffee
- 1/4 cup water
- 2 teaspoons pure vanilla extract
- 1 teaspoon apple cider or white vinegar
- 1/2 cup vegetable oil
- 1 cup Marshmallow Fluff
- 2 tablespoons unsalted butter, softened
- 1 tablespoon confectioner's sugar
- 1 tablespoon heavy cream
- a small handful of Red Hots cinnamon candies, finely crushed (optional)

### Direction

- Sweet Spice
- In a small sauté pan over low heat, stir spices until fragrant. Remove from heat and let cool. Store in a tightly-sealing glass jar.
- Alternatively, if using whole spices, stir in pan over low heat until fragrant. Let cool. Grind in a spice mill and store the mix in a tightly-sealing glass jar.
- Cake
- Preheat oven to 340 degrees F. Set oven rack to middle. Grease an 8" cake pan with cooking spray, then line with parchment and lightly spray the parchment. (This is in case you decide to remove cake from pan and frost completely. But usually we just frost the top and eat it right out of the pan.)
- Whisk flour, sugar, cocoa, baking soda, salt and spices in a medium bowl.
- In a measuring cup, mix together stout, coffee, water, vanilla and vinegar. Stir into the flour mixture a few turns, then add your oil and combine until you have a smooth batter.

- Pour into prepared pan. Place in oven and bake for 30 to 35 minutes. Check with cake tester, which should come out very slightly moist. Remove from oven and let cool on rack.
- FOR THE MARSHMALLOW BUTTERCREAM FROSTING: In a medium bowl, mix together the Fluff, butter, confectioner's sugar and cream using a hand blender on high speed until smooth. This quantity makes just enough to frost the top of the cake. Double the recipe if you want more.
- Turn cake out onto cake plate, if you're feeling fancy. Spread cake with frosting. Sprinkle crushed Red Hots over the frosting.

## 109. S'MORES SKILLET

*Serving: Serves 4 | Prep: | Cook: |Ready in:*

## Ingredients

- Marshmallows
- 12 ounces bag of Nestle's Milk Chocolate Morsels
- Box of Graham Crackers (this contains 3 individually wrapped packages of 9 graham crackers each)
- 3/4 stick softened butter (a little less than 1/2 cup)

## Direction

- Preheat oven to 350*F
- In a medium mixing bowl, crush together 1 package of 9 full graham crackers and 3/4 stick softened butter
- Cut each marshmallow in half (or use your fingers and pull them gently in half) and place cut half as next layer on top of milk chocolate morsels. Continue until entire cast iron skillet is covered
- Toast in oven for 10-15 minutes, until chocolate has melted and marshmallow is starting to toast

- Now, here comes the fun - you can either a. turn the broiler on low and keep a VERY close eye on marshmallows to toast or b. using a kitchen torch (which is what I use), gently toast the tops of the marshmallows
- Serve with graham crackers for dipping

## 110. S'Mores Pudding Cake

*Serving: Serves 8 or more | Prep: | Cook: |Ready in:*

## Ingredients

- S'Mores Pudding Cake
- 4 cups (1 batch) Rich Chocolate Custard (recipe below)
- 4 sleeves graham crackers
- 3 cups mini marshmallows
- 1 (13-ounce) jar marshmallow crème
- Rich Chocolate Custard
- 6 ounces semi-sweet or bittersweet chocolate, finely chopped
- 3 tablespoons cornstarch
- 1/4 teaspoon salt
- 1 cup cream
- 3 large egg yolks
- 1/2 cup sugar
- 2 cups whole milk
- 1 teaspoon pure vanilla extract

## Direction

- Smear a thin layer of chocolate custard in the center of a 9x13-inch baking dish. Cover the bottom with a layer of graham crackers and spread 1/3 (about 1 1/4 cups) of the chocolate custard on top of the crackers. Sprinkle 1 cup of mini marshmallows over the custard, and torch them lightly with a kitchen torch, until soft and browned. (You can also put them under an oven broiler for 45 seconds.) Repeat two more times and top with a final layer of graham crackers. (There will be four full layers of crackers, and three of pudding).

- Warm the marshmallow crème in the microwave or in a saucepan. Spread over the top of the icebox cake and spread while still warm. Refrigerate for at least 2 hours, or until the crackers have softened to a cakelike texture (test by inserting a thin knife along the side and bringing up a few crumbs). (This can be made up to 24 hours ahead of time, but it is best consumed with a day or two as it will get soggy if it sits too long.)
- When ready to serve, brown the top of the cake until tan and toasty with a kitchen torch or under the broiler.
- FOR THE CHOCOLATE CUSTARD: Prepare the chocolate: Place the chopped chocolate in a medium heatproof bowl.
- Make a cornstarch and egg slurry: Put the cornstarch and salt together in a medium bowl and whisk to make sure there are no lumps. Slowly whisk in the cream, making sure there are no lumps. (To be really sure, reach into the bowl and gently rub out any lumps between your fingers.) Whisk in the egg yolks.
- Warm the milk: In a 3-quart (2.8-L) saucepan over medium heat, whisk the sugar into the milk. Warm for 3 to 5 minutes, until the sugar dissolves, bubbles form around the edges, and the entire surface of the milk begins to quiver. Turn off the heat.
- Temper the slurry: Pour 1 cup (240 ml) of the hot milk into the bowl with the slurry, whisking constantly. The mixture should come together smoothly, with no lumps. If you see any, add a little more liquid and whisk them out. Pour it back into the pan, counting to 10 and whisking constantly as you pour.
- Thicken the pudding: Turn the heat back on to medium and bring the mixture to a simmer, whisking frequently and vigorously, working all the angles of the pot and scraping the bottom. Continue whisking for about 5 minutes, until the custard becomes very thick and starts to boil, with large bubbles that slowly pop up to the surface. Boil for 2 minutes, whisking constantly.
- Flavor the pudding: Turn off the heat and stir in the vanilla extract. Stir the chocolate into the pudding and let sit for 2 to 3 minutes. Whisk gently until the pudding is smooth and glossy and has fully absorbed the chocolate.
- Chill the pudding: Immediately pour the hot pudding into a shallow container. Place plastic wrap or buttered wax paper directly on the surface of the pudding (if you don't like pudding skin). Cover and refrigerate.

## 111. S'more Cookie Cups

*Serving: Serves 12 | Prep: | Cook: | Ready in:*

### Ingredients

- 3/4 cup flour
- 3/4 cup graham cracker crumbs
- 2 teaspoons corn starch
- 1/2 teaspoon baking soda
- 1/2 teaspoon salt
- 1/2 cup butter, softened
- 1/2 cup brown sugar
- 1/4 cup granulated sugar
- 1 teaspoon vanilla
- 1 egg
- 1 and 1/4 cups milk chocolate chips
- marshmallow creme

### Direction

- Heat oven to 375° F. Spray 12-count muffin pan with cooking spray and set aside.
- In small bowl combine flour, graham cracker crumbs, corn starch, baking soda, and salt.
- In large bowl beat butter, brown sugar, granulated sugar, and vanilla until creamy. Add egg and beat well. Gradually add in dry ingredients and mix well. Stir in chocolate chips.
- Use cookie scoop or tablespoon to add about two tablespoons of cookie dough to each muffin tin. Use hands to flatten dough. Add about one tablespoon of marshmallow crème on top of the dough. Evenly disperse the

remaining cookie dough and add on top of the marshmallow crème.
- Bake cookies 15 minutes or until golden brown. Let cool and use plastic knife to remove from muffin pan.

## 112. S'mores Angel Food Cake

*Serving: Serves 12 | Prep: | Cook: |Ready in:*

### Ingredients

- For the Cake
- 1.75 cups sugar
- 1/4 teaspoon salt
- 1 cup cake flour
- 12 egg whites, room temperature
- 1/3 cup warm water
- 1 teaspoon vanilla
- 1.5 teaspoons cream of tartar
- For Topping
- 12 ounces milk chocolate finely chopped
- 6 ounces heavy whipping cream
- 1 cup marshmallow fluff, store bought or homemade
- 1/2 cup graham cracker crumbs

### Direction

- Place sugar in a food processor and blend for two minutes, until sugar becomes very fine.
- In a medium bowl, combine cake flour, salt, and half of the fine sugar. Sift together and set aside.
- Preheat oven to 350°F.
- Combine egg whites, water, vanilla and cream of tartar in the bowl of your stand mixer. Whisk ingredients together for 2 minutes until well combined. Gradually add remaining half of sugar and Beat egg white mixture until medium peaks are formed.
- Sprinkle some of the flour mixture over the top of egg white mixture. Gently fold in. Repeat until all of the flour mixture has been folded in evenly.
- Spoon mixture into an ungreased tube pan and bake for 35-40 minutes, until golden brown in color and cake is cooked through.
- Invert cake pan and cool upside down (cake remaining in the pan) until completely cooled.
- Once cooled, run a knife along the inside tube and the outside to loosen the cake. Lift the tube from the rest of the pan and invert the cake onto a cooling rack, using the knife to loosen it from the bottom, if necessary.
- To make the ganache
- Finely chop chocolate and place in a bowl. Bring cream just barely to a simmer and pour over chopped chocolate. Cover with plastic wrap and let stand 2 mins. Stir with a spatula until combined and smooth.
- Allow the ganache to cool a bit before using.
- Place the cooling rack with cake on top over the top of your sink. Pour the ganache over the cake, spreading evenly over the sides, top, and inside.
- Take the graham cracker crumbs and throw them along the bottom half of the cake. This is the best way I can describe this.
- Spread or pipe marshmallow crème over the top of the cake. Carefully toast the top with a culinary torch.

## 113. S'mores Cookie Dough Bites

*Serving: Serves 24 | Prep: | Cook: |Ready in:*

### Ingredients

- 1 stick unsalted butter, room temperature
- ¾ cups light brown sugar, lightly packed
- ½ teaspoons vanilla extract
- Pinch of salt
- ½ cups all-purpose flour
- ½ cups graham cracker crumbs, plus more for sprinkling
- 24 miniature marshmallows
- 1 cup chocolate chips

## Direction

- Beat the butter and sugar in the bowl of an electric mixer until light and fluffy. Add the vanilla and salt and mix until combined.
- Put the flour into a large frying pan over medium heat. Toast the flour, stirring constantly, until it has a light golden color and a nutty fragrance.
- Add the flour and graham cracker crumbs to the butter and mix until combined. Divide the cookie dough into 24 equal portions.
- Place the marshmallows on a baking sheet and gently toast them with a kitchen blowtorch. Turn the marshmallows over and toast the other side.
- When the marshmallows have cooled, use your hands to wrap one piece of cookie dough around each miniature marshmallow. When all of the cookie dough bites have been rolled, place them on a waxed paper-lined sheet pan in the refrigerator to chill for 1 hour or more.
- When the cookie dough bites are thoroughly chilled, melt the chocolate chips. Dip the chilled cookie dough into the chocolate, shaking off any excess. Place the chocolate-dipped bites onto the waxed paper-lined sheet pan, sprinkling the tops with graham cracker crumbs as you go. Allow the chocolate to harden in the refrigerator before serving.

## 114. THE BEST BANANA BUTTERSCOTCH ICE CREAM EVER

Serving: Serves 12 large scoops | Prep: | Cook: | Ready in:

## Ingredients

- For the sauce
- 2-1/2 medium ripe bananas (not green, brown, or squishy)
- 4 tablespoons salted butter, coarsely chopped
- 1/2 cup dark brown sugar, packed
- 1/2 cup heavy whipping cream
- For the ice cream
- 1 pint heavy whipping cream
- 7 ounces container, marshmallow cream
- 1/4 teaspoon banana extract
- 3/4 cup walnuts
- some banana chips, GARNISH

## Direction

- Peel bananas, cut in half. Cut all bananas lengthwise 2 times, and into 1/2-inch pieces, and set aside.
- Prepare butterscotch sauce -- in medium saucepan on high, bring butter, sugar, and cream to a boil. Boil on medium for 3 minutes, stirring occasionally. Add banana pieces and stir gently with rubber spatula for 1 minute. Pour into large bowl and place in freezer for 10 minutes to cool a little.
- Prepare ice cream -- chop walnuts, set aside. Place cream, marshmallow fluff, and extract into food processor. (Dip rubber spatula into cream for easy removal of marshmallow.) Depending on cream, process for 10-20 seconds or until almost thick or soft peaks. Add walnuts; press down and swirl round with spatula to combine.
- Pour this marshmallow cream mixture into 9 X 13 inch pan. Remove sauce bowl from freezer and spoon mixture on top. Gently fold into portions of the cream (do not combine everything together, leave like ripples). Cover with foil and place in freezer until consistency of ice cream, about 4 to 6 hours.
- To serve, place a large scoop or two of ice cream in a colorful bowl, sherbet glass, fancy martini glass, or your choice. Garnish each scoop with optional 2 banana chips in the center. And, of course, there's always that bold and beautiful old fashioned ice cream cone.

## 115. The Best Chocolate Brownies From Scratch

*Serving: Makes 18-20 | Prep: | Cook: |Ready in:*

### Ingredients

- 4 large eggs
- 1 1/2 cups pure maple syrup
- 2 teaspoons vanilla
- 1 1/2 cups hard white wheat flour
- 3/4 cup vegetable oil
- 1 tablespoon vegetable oil
- 1/2 cup cocoa powder
- 2 tablespoons cocoa powder
- 1/3 cup brown lentils, cooked
- 1 cup small marshmallows

### Direction

- Pre-heat oven to 350°. Grease 9X13 pan.
- Beat eggs and maple syrup together. Add in oil and vanilla.
- Sift together Hard White Wheat flour, cocoa and salt then slowly add to egg mixture and stir well, or beat in mixer on medium speed for approximately 1.5 minutes, (you will know when well blended).
- Stir in cooked lentils, chocolate chips, and marshmallows and continue stirring/mixing until well blended. Immediately transfer to baking dish.
- Bake at 350° for 35 minutes. Let cool before serving.
- In a chilled bowl whip heavy whipping cream. Add a dollop to each serving. Or if you prefer, ice cream is also a great way to top off our delicious lentil brownies.

## 116. Tropical Ambrosia

*Serving: Serves 2 or more | Prep: | Cook: |Ready in:*

### Ingredients

- 2 tablespoons sour cream
- 2 tablespoons heavy cream, whipped to stiff peaks (optional)
- 1 tablespoon brown sugar
- 1 teaspoon lime juice
- 1 cup mango, chopped
- 1 cup pineapple, chopped
- 1 kiwi, chopped
- 2 tablespoons shredded coconut, or more to taste
- 2 mint leaves, sliced into thin ribbons (optional)
- 1/2 cup mini marshmallows (optional)
- 1 tablespoon flaked coconut, toasted
- 1/4 teaspoon poppy seeds or chia seeds (optional)
- finely grated lime zest, just a sprinkle over top

### Direction

- Fold together the sour cream, whipped cream, brown sugar and lime juice.
- In a medium bowl, toss fruit with shredded coconut. Fold in cream mixture. Fold in mint and marshmallows, if using. Chill. When ready to serve, sprinkle poppy seeds and flaked coconut over top. Finish with a little grated lime zest.

## 117. Vanilla Marshmallow Creme Brulee

*Serving: Serves 6 | Prep: | Cook: |Ready in:*

### Ingredients

- 1 quart Heavy cream
- 1 Vanilla bean, split and scraped
- 6 Egg yolks
- 1/2 cup Marshmallow creme
- Sugar for topping

### Direction

- Preheat oven to 325 degrees. Bring the cream, split vanilla bean, and vanilla seeds just to a boil in a pot over medium heat. Remove from heat and let stand for a few minutes.
- In a mixing bowl, combine the egg yolks with marshmallow crème and beat until smooth.
- Remove the split vanilla bean from the cream. Slowly incorporate the cream into the egg mixture while continually whisking.
- Pour into 6 (8-ounce) ramekins and place them in a roasting pan. Pour enough hot water into the pan to come halfway up the sides of the ramekins, creating a water bath.
- Bake for 45-50 minutes so that the crème brûlées are set but still a bit wobbly in the middle, and then remove them from the water bath. Refrigerate them for a few hours or overnight.
- Before serving, sprinkle each ramekin with a thin layer of sugar and caramelize using either the oven broiler or kitchen blow torch. If broiling, keep an eye on them and rotate as necessary. You may also need to refrigerate them for a few hours in order to reset the crème brûlées.
- Serve with fresh fruit, whipped cream, toasted marshmallows, or all of the above and enjoy!

## 118. Vegan Rocky Road Ice Cream

*Serving: Serves 6 | Prep: | Cook: | Ready in:*

## Ingredients

- 30 ounces organic coconut milk (Full fat is best!)
- 1/2 cup granulated sugar
- 1/2 cup cocoa powder
- 1 teaspoon pure vanilla extract
- 1 1/2 teaspoons arrowroot
- 1 cup unsalted roasted almonds, chopped
- 1 cup vegan mini marshmallows (Dandie's makes an awesome, easy-to-find option!)

## Direction

- In a medium stockpot, add your coconut milk, sugar, cocoa powder and vanilla. Bring this mixture to a light simmer over medium heat, whisking vigorously to make sure the sugar is dissolved and the cocoa powder is evenly incorporated. (The heat should make these ingredients meld together pretty seamlessly, but it's normal to note a bit of separation.)
- Put a few tablespoons (two to three) of your warm mixture into a small bowl. Add your arrowroot and whisk together until completely smooth.
- Add the arrowroot mixture back to your base. Whisk together for about one minute more and then remove from heat.
- Transfer your ice cream base to a large bowl and refrigerate for about 3-4 hours or up to overnight. Once completely chilled, it's time to churn: add to your ice cream maker of choice and follow the given instructions for your appliance. (If you're using the KitchenAid Ice Cream Maker attachment, like me, the churning will take about 15-20 minutes on a medium speed.)
- Transfer your ice cream to a freezer safe container, layering your chopped almonds and marshmallows throughout. More your container to the very back of your freezer to harden completely. This should take about 4-6 hours, depending on the coldness of your freezer.
- The last step is the most important one: scoop into bowls or cones, enjoy and let your world be rocked - get it?

## 119. Vegetable

*Serving: Serves 6 | Prep: | Cook: | Ready in:*

## Ingredients

- 3 oranges
- 3 cups mashed sweet potatoes

- 1/4 cup brown sugar
- 1/2 cup orange juice
- 2 tablespoons butter
- 1/2 teaspoon salt
- 24 tiny marshmallows

## Direction

- Cut oranges in half making a jagged up and down edge (www). Remove pulp and membranes to make 6 orange cups. Squeeze the pulp and save 1/2 cup for orange juice.
- Combine sweet potatoes, brown sugar, butter, salt and orange juice. Mix well and fill orange shells with the potato mixture. Decorate with 4 marshmallow on each. Bake at 350 degrees for 1 hour.

- Press mixture into prepared pan and bake for 20 minutes until golden.
- Spread warm base with jam.
- Cover with marshmallows, flat side facing down.
- Bake for 2 minutes or until marshmallow has slightly melted.
- Remove from oven. Cool in tin.
- Combine chocolate and remaining butter in small saucepan over low heat.
- Cook, stirring until melted, then pour over marshmallows.
- Tap pan to level surface.
- Refrigerate for 2 hours or until set.
- Stand at room temperature for 5 minutes before cutting into pieces and serving.

## 120. Wagon Wheel Slice

*Serving: Makes 12 | Prep: | Cook: | Ready in:*

### Ingredients

- 250 grams Organic Times salted butter, softened.
- 1/3 cup caster sugar
- 1 1/2 cups plain flour
- 3/4 cup raspberry jam
- 150 grams Organic Times vanilla mallows (marshmallows) halved longways
- 300 grams Organic Times dark chocolate drops

### Direction

- Preheat oven to 180°C/160°C fan-forced.
- Grease a 3cm-deep, medium size rectangular slice pan.
- Line base and sides with baking paper, extending paper 2cm from edge on all sides.
- Using an electric mixer, beat 200g butter and sugar until light and fluffy.
- Sift flours over butter mixture. Stir until dough comes together.

## 121. Waldorf Salad

*Serving: Serves 4 | Prep: | Cook: | Ready in:*

### Ingredients

- 4 tart apples, washed and cut into large cubes with the peel left on
- 2-3 celery stalks, cut into thin half-moon slices
- 3/4 cup pecans, broken into large pieces
- 1/2 cup mini marshmallows
- 4 ounces cream cheese
- orange juice

### Direction

- Combine the apple pieces, sliced celery, pecan pieces, and mini marshmallows in a large bowl.
- In a smaller bowl, beat the cream cheese until soft and smooth. Gradually beat in orange juice until you have the right consistency for a dressing.
- Pour the cream cheese/orange juice dressing over your salad. Toss. Chill in the refrigerator (the acid in the orange juice will keep the apple pieces from turning brown.

## 122. White Chocolate Rocky Road

*Serving: Makes 12 large bars or 24 medium bars | Prep: | Cook: | Ready in:*

### Ingredients

- 18 ounces high quality marshmallows (such as Williams-Sonoma handcrafted marshmallows, or make your own)
- 2.5 pounds Valrhona white chocolate
- 1 pound whole raw pistachios (unsalted)
- 16 ounces natural flavored gummy candies (I used Bissinger's Pomegranate flavored Gummy Panda's)

### Direction

- Roast the pistachios at 250F for about 10 - 15 minutes, or until golden. Be sure to check them, so they do not burn.
- Chop the marshmallows into bite sized pieces (if you're using large marshmallows) - I used kitchen scissors.
- Melt the white chocolate over a double boiler stirring constantly, or use the microwave. Ensure the chocolate is chopped into pieces, and then put the chocolate on a medium heat setting for about 3 minutes, stirring in between each minute of cooking. Once about 50% of the chocolate is melted, the rest will melt if you remove the chocolate from the microwave and continue to stir. Be careful not to burn the chocolate, as there is no way to 'recover' except starting over.
- In a large bowl, mix the whole, roasted pistachios, the chopped marshmallows and gummy candies. Pour over the melted chocolate and mix quickly to combine.
- Pour into a lined brownie pan (9x11) and refrigerate for several hours, until set.
- Once set, remove the pan from the fridge, and take the chocolate out of the pan. I like to slice the chocolate into bars, this gives a view of the green pistachios and red candies, amongst the white chocolate and marshmallows. I then wrap the bars in clear cellophane and tie the ends with ribbons to give as gifts. You could also cut the rocky road into bite-sized squares and box up to give as gifts.
- Note: Although it may be tempting to use a cheaper chocolate, the quality of this dish is really determined by the chocolate. I recommend Valrhona, or you could try another high quality chocolate such as Lindt. This makes a huge difference to the dish.

## 123. Fluffer Nutter Brownies

*Serving: Makes 16 | Prep: | Cook: | Ready in:*

### Ingredients

- 1 stick + 2 tablespoons unsalted butter
- 1 cup granulated sugar
- 3/4 cup 2 tablespoons unsweetened cocoa powder
- 1/4 teaspoon salt
- 1 teaspoon vanilla extract
- 2 large eggs
- 1/2 cup all purpose flour
- 1/2 cup 1 tablespoon peanut butter chips
- 1/2 cup 1 tablespoon chocolate chips (I used miniature chips)
- 1/2 cup 1 tablespoon miniature marshmallows
- 1/2 cup 1 tablespoon chopped salted peanuts

### Direction

- Preheat oven to 325 degrees. Spray the bottom and sides of an 8" square pan with vegetable spray. Line the bottom of the pan with parchment paper, leaving an overhang on either side to assist in lifting the brownies from the pan. Set aside.
- Into a large glass or other microwave safe bowl, add the butter, granulated sugar, cocoa

powder and salt. Heat in the microwave in 30 second increments until the butter is melted. Stir until the mixture is completely combined. Set aside to cool while you assemble the other ingredients.
- Stir in the vanilla extract and add the eggs, one at a time, stirring after each addition. Add the flour and stir until just combined. Add the half cup of peanut butter chips, chocolate chips, miniature marshmallows and peanuts. Fold into the batter. Pour into the baking pan and smooth the top with a spatula. Sprinkle the remaining 1 tablespoon of the chips marshmallows and peanuts on top of the brownies. Lightly press them into the batter with your fingertips.
- Bake for 25-30 minutes and check for doneness with a cake tester or toothpick. If it comes out with just a few crumbs, the brownies are done. If you cook them too long, they'll be more cake-y than fudgy. If the batter is still liquidy, cook for an additional 3-5 minutes.
- Let the brownies cool to room temperature. Run a knife around the edges and gently lift them from the pan onto a cutting board. Use a long, sharp knife to cut them into squares.
- Store in an airtight container.

# Index

## A
Allspice 43
Almond 3,6,7,15,19,39,46

## B
Bacon 3,4,5,45
Baking 26,43,45
Banana 3,6,21,38
Berry 3,5
Bran 40
Bread 47
Brown sugar 49
Buckwheat 47
Butter 3,4,6,7,13,22,29,35,38,39,40,46,49,58,59,60,64

## C
Cake 3,4,27,33,37,42,44,47,53,54,58,64,67,68,70
Cashew 3,14
Champ 3,8
Cheese 3,4,17,18,35,36,50,62
Cherry 3,17
Chips 3,5,9,13,19,43
Chocolate 3,4,5,6,7,8,9,10,11,13,15,16,18,21,25,28,31,32,34,35,36,40,41,43,46,50,59,63,68,72,75
Cinnamon 3,6,8,11,29,43
Cloves 43
Cocktail 39
Cocoa powder 36
Coconut 3,12,14
Coffee 3,13

Crackers 22,68
Cream 3,4,6,10,11,14,15,16,18,22,28,31,32,39,44,47,48,53,59,73
Croissant 4,52,53
Custard 64,68

## D
Dark chocolate 8,53

## E
Egg 45,72

## F
Flour 3,16,29,43
Fruit 3,18,19
Fudge 3,15,18,32

## G
Grain 67

## H
Honey 3,25,40,46

## I
Ice cream 22
Icing 23,63

## J
Jelly 3,40
Jus 15,45,65

## L
Lemon 3,31,34,35

## M
Macaroon 43
Marshmallow 1,3,4,5,6,7,8,9,18,19,20,22,25,27,28,30,31,32,33,34,36,39,40,42,43,45,48,59,67,68,72
Mascarpone 34

Meringue 3,31

Milk 4,6,7,9,13,22,45,47,53,68

Mint 3,35

# N

Nut 3,4,7,18,19,29,38,43,45,75

# O

Oatmeal 3,29

Oats 40

Oil 29,30

Olive 29

Orange 60

# P

Peach 59

Peanuts 39

Pecan 30,36

Peel 8,28,61,71

Pepper 3,4,27,28,30,32,40,41

Pie 3,4,5,10,22,24,25,29,30,31,33,44,55,56

Pomegranate 75

Popcorn 3,4,6,30,42,60

Potato 3,4,8,12,29,35,46,65,66

Pulse 67

Pumpkin 4,42,43,44

# R

Raspberry 59

Rice 3,4,5,6,7,9,11,12,14,19,20,35,39,40,41,42,45,46,62

# S

Salad 4,74

Salt 3,4,6,16,19,30,35,43,49,59

Seeds 6

Soda 43

Sponge cake 31

Squash 3,22

Strawberry 4,59,62

Sugar 29,36,42,43,49,72

Syrup 34

# T

Toffee 3,4,13,42,43,47,59

Tomato 3,17

Turkish delight 20

# V

Vanilla extract 49

Vegan 4,73

# W

Walnut 3,8,13

# Z

Zest 66

# Conclusion

Thank you again for downloading this book!

I hope you enjoyed reading about my book!

If you enjoyed this book, please take the time to share your thoughts and post a review on Amazon. It'd be greatly appreciated!

Write me an honest review about the book – I truly value your opinion and thoughts and I will incorporate them into my next book, which is already underway.

Thank you!

If you have any questions, **feel free to contact at:** author@sauterecipes.com

Wendy Beran

sauterecipes.com

Printed in Great Britain
by Amazon